PE1011
.E928

41,516

D0629362

╔══════════════════════════╗

BASILEIAD

LIBRARY

❦

MANOR JUNIOR COLLEGE

FOX CHASE MANOR

JENKINTOWN, PA. 19046

WITHDRAWN

PRESENTED BY

MANOR JUNIOR COLLEGE

LIBRARY FUND

╚══════════════════════════╝

George Fitzmaurice

THE IRISH WRITERS SERIES
James F. Carens, General Editor

EIMAR O'DUFFY	Robert Hogan
J. C. MANGAN	James Kilroy
J. M. SYNGE	Robin Skelton
PAUL VINCENT CARROLL	Paul A. Doyle
SEAN O'CASEY	Bernard Benstock
SEUMAS O'KELLY	George Brandon Saul
SHERIDAN LEFANU	Michael Begnal
SOMERVILLE AND ROSS	John Cronin
STANDISH O'GRADY	Phillip L. Marcus
SUSAN L. MITCHELL	Richard M. Kain
W. R. RODGERS	Darcy O'Brien
MERVYN WALL	Robert Hogan
LADY GREGORY	Hazard Adams
LIAM O'FLAHERTY	James O'Brien
MARIA EDGEWORTH	James Newcomer
SIR SAMUEL FERGUSON	Malcolm Brown
BRIAN FRIEL	D. E. S. Maxwell
PEADAR O'DONNELL	Grattan Freyer
DANIEL CORKERY	George Brandon Saul
BENEDICT KIELY	Daniel Casey
CHARLES ROBERT MATURIN	Robert E. Lougy
DOUGLAS HYDE	Gareth Dunleavy
EDNA O'BRIEN	Grace Eckley
FRANCIS STUART	J. H. Natterstad
JOHN BUTLER YEATS	Douglas N. Archibald
JOHN MONTAGUE	Frank Kersnowski
KATHARINE TYNAN	Marilyn Gaddis Rose
BRIAN MOORE	Jeanne Flood
PATRICK KAVANAGH	Darcy O'Brien
OLIVER ST. JOHN GOGARTY	J. B. Lyons
GEORGE FITZMAURICE	Arthur McGuinness

GEORGE FITZMAURICE

Arthur E. McGuinness

Lewisburg
BUCKNELL UNIVERSITY PRESS
London: ASSOCIATED UNIVERSITY PRESSES

41,516

©1975 by Associated University Presses, Inc.

Associated University Presses, Inc.
Cranbury, New Jersey 08512

Associated University Presses
108 New Bond Street
London W1Y OQX, England

Library of Congress Cataloging in Publication Data

McGuinness, Arthur E.
   George Fitzmaurice.

   (The Irish writers series)
   Bibliography: p.
   1. Fitzmaurice, George.
PR6011.I9Z8   822   72-168815
ISBN 0-8387-7870-4
ISBN 0-8387-7980-8 (pbk.)

For Nora, who already knows about Kerry,
and for Katie, who will learn.

Printed in the United States of America

Contents

Chronology

1877	January 28. George Fitzmaurice born in Bedford House, a few miles north of Listowel, Co. Kerry.
1900	His short stories begin appearing in Dublin weeklies where he would continue to publish until 1907.
1901	Gets a "temporary clerkship" in Dublin. He spent the next 41 years in civil service jobs.
1907	October 3. *The Country Dressmaker* produced at the Abbey Theatre, the same year as *The Playboy of the Western World.* Yeats anticipated a repeat of the riots.
1908	March 19. *The Pie-Dish* produced at the Abbey.
1912	Abbey revival of *The Country Dressmaker.* The first full-length play to be revived by the theater. The play became the fifth most frequently performed play in the Abbey's repertoire.
1913	Abbey Theatre production of *The Magic Glasses.*
1914	*Five Plays* published by Maunsel in Dublin.

Contained *The Country Dressmaker, The Moonlighter, The Pie-Dish, The Magic Glasses,* and *The Dandy Dolls.*

1914-18 Fitzmaurice served with Army in France.

1923   *'Twixt the Giltinans and the Carmodys* produced at the Abbey. The theater accepted no more Fitzmaurice plays for production until 1969, after the dramatist's death.

1924-57 Eight Fitzmaurice plays published in Seumas O'Sullivan's *Dublin Magazine. The Enchanted Land* occupied an entire issue in 1957.

1942   Retires from the Civil Service at age 65. Continues to live in Dublin until his death.

1945   *The Dandy Dolls* produced by Austin Clarke's Lyric Theatre Company.

1948   *The Moonlighter* produced by Liam Miller at the Peacock Theatre.

1949   *The Linnaun Shee,* published in 1924, produced by the Lyric Theatre Company.

1952   First production of *One Evening Gleam.*

1953   First production of *There are Tragedies and Tragedies.*

1963   May 12. George Fitzmaurice dies alone at age 86 in Dublin rooming house.

1967-70 Dolmen Press publication of three-volume *Plays of George Fitzmaurice* and of short stories.

1969   Abbey Theatre production of *The Dandy Dolls.*

George Fitzmaurice

1

"Parson Fitzmaurice's Son George"

To enter the world of George Fitzmaurice, one must understand that it is a fair distance from Listowel to Abbeyfeale and a long journey from Abbeyfeale to Castleisland. Fitzmaurice's plays are mostly about the Kingdom of Kerry, a region which Kerrymen grudgingly admit may also be called County Kerry. Whether this part of the world belongs to something larger called Ireland is questionable. The world of Kerry is bounded on the north by Clare and Limerick, on the south and east by Cork, and on the west by the sea. All are foreign places, as far away in the Kerry consciousness as Dublin, London, or America. Only the unfortunate or the foolish leave Kerry and Kerrymen pray nightly for their return.

Fitzmaurice country in North Kerry does not have the romantic topography of the County Kerry one sees in tourist books: high, craggy mountains their summits shrouded in mist, rocky coastline battered by the sea, blue lakes sparkling in the valleys and mountain passes. The spectacular scenery of the Dingle peninsula changes as one moves north into Fitzmaurice country away from the sea, the lakes, and the mountains. The rolling farmland, divided by furze hedges and grey stone walls into a multitude of fields, still supports the industry of the dairy farmers who people Fitzmaurice's plays. These men can yet be seen taking the day's milk to the creamery in their horse-drawn wagons.

Fitzmaurice does not romanticize these Kerry folk. He knows them as a violent people who barely survive their daily battle with nature. He presents them as a stubborn and insensitive lot who compound the problems in their lives with petty bickering and unforgiving natures. But, as a Kerryman himself, he knows too the lyricism of their dialect and he can reproduce this North Kerry dialect with the accuracy of a native speaker. And he knows the supernaturalism which is a part of their lives and expresses itself most frequently in the conflict between Christianity and the older traditional folklore.

Fitzmaurice wrote seventeen plays and had the reputation early in his career of being one of the Irish theater's most significant folk-dramatists, a distinction he shared with Lady Gregory, Synge, and Padraic Colum. In *Contemporary Drama of Ireland (1917)* Ernest Boyd wrote that "George Fitzmaurice has ... imagination and style of a sufficiently personal quality to give him rank as the greatest folk-dramatist since the death of J. M. Synge, and the practical withdrawal of Colum's plays from the current repertory of the Abbey Theatre." But he died at the age of eighty-six in 1963 in nearly total obscurity. The Abbey Theatre had produced his *Country Dressmaker* in 1907, soon after *The Playboy of the Western World,* and Yeats had

anticipated a repeat of the *Playboy* riots, since Fitzmaurice's play was even closer to the Irish peasant
experience than Synge's. *The Country Dressmaker*
would become the fifth most revived and performed
play in the Abbey's repertoire. Other Abbey productions of his plays followed, *The Pie-Dish* in 1908, *The
Magic Glasses* in 1913, and *'Twixt the Giltinans and
the Carmodys* in 1923. After this, however, no more
Fitzmaurice plays were staged by the Abbey during his
lifetime. While there were occasional productions by
groups like the Lyric Theatre Company in the years
after World War II Fitzmaurice was by then an all—but—
forgotten dramatist.

More recent critics have puzzled over the neglect of
Fitzmaurice's plays. In the most perceptive essay yet
written on the dramatist (*The London Magazine*, February, 1965), Irving Wardle speculated that their neglect
did not originate in a quarrel between Yeats and Fitzmaurice, as some have thought, but simply that Fitzmaurice was consistently unfashionable. "After *The
Country Dressmaker*. . . he was out of step with the
times; producing somber works when audiences wanted
comedy, bizarre fantasies when realism came into fash-
ion, and anticipating O'Casey in tragi-comedy by nearly twenty years."

When Fitzmaurice died in a Dublin rooming house at
3 Harcourt St., his literary remains were found in a
single battered suitcase containing copies of his published plays and manuscripts of some unpublished plays.
His meager library did not even include a copy of *Five
Plays,* the only collection of his plays published in his
lifetime. Alongside his bed the following note was found

written in pencil: "Author is prepared to sell outright all rights in 14 plays dealing intimately with life in the Irish countryside. Most have already been either printed or published. Suitable to which to build musical, television, etc. Pass to anyone interested." A tragic fate indeed for one who may have succeeded best of all Irish dramatists in capturing the quality of life in the west, especially the vitality of its dialect.

In the decade since his death, fate has been a bit kinder to George Fitzmaurice and he will soon again be recognized as a significant part of the history of Irish folk drama. In 1967, a collected edition of all of Fitzmaurice's plays was published by Dolmen Press, thus making most of his plays accessible to readers for the first time. (All subsequent quotations from Fitzmaurice's plays are from this edition and will be cited in the text by volume and page number.) The Abbey Theatre produced *The Dandy Dolls* in 1969. Other North Kerry writers, most notably John B. Keane and Bryan MacMahon, speak warmly of Fitzmaurice's plays and their accurate expression of Kerry life. The annual Listowel Writers' Week has focused critical attention on Fitzmaurice. A world premiere of his farce *The Toothache* was done at the 1973 Writers' Week. In addition to the present study, another book, *George Fitzmaurice and His Enchanted Land,* appeared in 1972. And the second number of the new *Journal of Irish Literature* (May, 1972) featured essays on the Listowel writers, including two on Fitzmaurice.

This comparative flurry of work on Fitzmaurice gives us a much better notion of his plays, but what of Fitzmaurice himself? The known facts are frustratingly few.

Fitzmaurice kept no diary and only a handful of his letters survive. A bachelor, he lived in Dublin for over half a century as a recluse with no close friends. He avoided the legitimate theater which had so neglected his works and instead frequented the shows at music halls where his anonymity could be assured. He is remembered in Dublin as a wiry little old man who loved to spend his leisure hours drinking Guinness in Mooney's and a few other favorite pubs. Fitzmaurice apparently never engaged in that honored Irish pastime of buying rounds. Even in the pub he could, therefore, be the uninvolved observer.

The place to begin the search for George Fitzmaurice, however, is not in Dublin pubs, but in the North Kerry farmlands and villages from which Fitzmaurice drew the characters and themes of his plays. There one finds social conditions which may well have reinforced Fitzmaurice's naturally shy personality. Indeed his relation to the Kerry folk was not the ordinary one. As Howard K. Slaughter has noted, he was a member of the gentry. He came from a family which goes back to the 1300s in *Burke's Landed Irish Gentry,* and which was Protestant in a part of Ireland overwhelmingly Roman Catholic. His father was a Church of Ireland clergyman who married a Catholic wife. It is uncertain whether the elder Fitzmaurice actually served in the Listowel parish, but if he did, his congregation would have numbered less than a dozen families. *Slater's Directory* for Listowel in 1881 defines the social hierachy of the town shortly after the dramatist's birth. The Rev. George Fitzmaurice is at the top of the list among "Gentry and Clergy." The list then goes on to less dignified stations, apothecaries, bakers, butchers, farmers, saddlers, nailers, etc. The combination of being Protestant and being gentry—living at the Great House, as Fitzmaurice himself would put it in his play *The Moonlighter*—effectively separated young George Fitzmaurice from a social life in the community. In later life he would find community in pubs which could offer to a man like Fitzmaurice a social leveling.

Fitzmaurice's family became land-poor after his father's death and this may also have contributed to his shy and withdrawn personality. His sisters lived on as spinsters in the family house, trying to keep up the appearance of gentility without sufficient money or expertise to work the land. I recently met a Mrs. Mc-Carthy, who lives across the river from the Fitzmaurice lands in Kilcara. She remembers the family as good people "even though they were Protestant," and she recalled with fondness being invited across the river of an afternoon to hear "Miss Una and Miss Georgine," George's sisters, play the piano. She remembers the array of cut flowers always present in the living room. The gentry remain gentry despite ill fortune. When I questioned Mr. Relihan, the farmer who currently owns the Fitzmaurice land, he remarked on the number of trees which the Fitzmaurice's had planted around the house. He felt they just used up good farming land.

George Fitzmaurice was born in Bedford House, a few miles north of Listowel, on January 28, 1877. He was the tenth of twelve children. The Fitzmaurice estate included several hundred acres of land which border on the Gale River, a tributary of the larger Feale River that connects Listowel and Abbeyfeale. Only about half of the original 1775 family house is now standing, but one still has the impression that it was owned by a well-to-do family. Set back off the road a good distance, the house must be approached through an iron gate and around a gravel crescent. The interior of the house is kept in fine condition by the Relihan family who live there now, and one finds the high ceilings and generally Georgian style which graces the finest Irish country houses. The house still has no central heating and peat is burned in the large fireplaces just as it was when George Fitzmaurice lived there.

When Fitzmaurice's father died in 1891, his mother did not have enough money left to pay a £60 butcher's bill and so was forced to give up the house as collateral. The family never managed to get the house back and moved, when George was a boy, to a smaller house on the River Feale near the village of Duagh. The family quite obviously was not poor at the time, since the new house had several large fields attached to it which probably ran to over a hundred acres.

Fitzmaurice's large family included seven sisters and four brothers, nearly half of whom died in infancy or early maturity and none of whom ever married. George was not interested or could not make a living with the family farm, so he left North Kerry for Cork City at about the age of twenty to work in a bank. He had finished what school there was in Duagh, but would be largely self-educated. He managed to get a "temporary clerkship" in 1901 which sent him to Dublin and the beginning of a long and not distinguished career in the civil service. He would not get permanent status until 1925, when he was forty-eight years old, and he did not reach full salary potential until 1935, when he was fifty-eight.

Little is known about his early interest in drama before the production of *The Country Dressmaker,* some six years after he arrived in Dublin. Robert Hogan's recent edition of Fitzmaurice's short stories reveals that Fitzmaurice began publishing fiction in Dublin weeklies in 1900. In these short stories Fitzmaurice tries to combine formal English and Kerry dialect with rather unfortunate results. The effect is that of an urbane and educated narrator recording the quaint illiteracies of peasants. Fitzmaurice needed a form in which dialect could function independent of any other style. *The Country Dressmaker,* his first Abbey play, was a reworking of one of these stories, "Maeve's Grand Lover." Fitzmaurice transformed this bit of minor fiction into one of the Abbey's most popular plays.

Fitzmaurice may have written some plays before *The Country Dressmaker,* but all one can do is speculate about this. Dating the composition of his plays is extremely difficult, since he left no journal or letters and the internal evidence is meager. The manuscripts he had in his suitcase when he died may very well have been his earliest plays. Professor Howard Slaughter thinks one of these, *The Toothache,* was Fitzmaurice's earliest script and that another, *The King of the Barna Men,* was the full-length play Joseph Holloway says Fitzmaurice submitted to the Abbey in 1906, the year before *The Country Dressmaker* was produced. This play was rejected by the Abbey and was never published or performed in Fitzmaurice's lifetime.

In *The Country Dressmaker* Fitzmaurice tones down

the rowdyism and violence of the two earlier plays and produces a play in which the Kerry character is generalized into conventional Irish types. He completely removes the supernaturalism, lyricism, and grotesquerie which run through his best plays and ends up with a decent comedy. Fitzmaurice knew that to be successful on the Abbey stage he had to normalize the real peasant character, and restrain his own imaginative exuberance. He wrote only three more plays which the Abbey would find "acceptable" Kerry folk-plays. One of these, *'Twixt the Giltinans and the Carmodys,* was a lesser version of *The Country Dressmaker,* again a conventional comedy. The other two, *The Pie-Dish* and *The Magic Glasses,* were different kinds of plays, full of darkness, violence, blasphemy, and death, as well as broad Kerry humor. Critics objected to these plays as not being proper comedies and they had very short runs, though *The Pie-Dish* was included in the repertoire on Abbey tours to England in 1909, 1910, and 1911. Fitzmaurice would have fared better today with an audience which has been educated by Beckett, Brecht, and Ionesco. As it was, when he didn't succeed at the Abbey, he was finished. Today a playwright like John B. Keane can ignore the Abbey and count on performances elsewhere in Dublin or in Cork or in Kerry itself. Fitzmaurice had no such possibilities.

All of this aside, the production of *The Country Dressmaker* must have been extremely gratifying to the thirty-year-old playwright. Joseph Holloway commented:

A large, fashionable and most appreciative audience

assembled to do the new playwright justice, and give his
first staged work an attentive and unprejudiced hearing.
The comedy was not long on its way when it was easy
to see that Fitzmaurice had a real grip of his subject and
that his dialogue was the real article and his men and
women those one might meet any day down in Kerry.
Two natives from Kerry sat before me and assured me
that the turn of phrase of the Kerry people was aptly
copied, and that the types were perfect specimens of the
ordinary folk to be met down there. "Even the very
names of the characters are Kerry to the backbone."

Holloway reports Fitzmaurice in attendance on opening
night, October 3, 1907, a fact which would not be
remarkable except that the playwright never again
attended a premiere of his plays. Shy to a fault, he
needed the psychological support of producers, actors,
and audience. He never again felt he had such support.
Critics reacted favorably to *The Country Dressmaker*
and it was eventually performed 181 times at the
Abbey.

Despite his longevity, George Fitzmaurice was frequently ill. A liver ailment caused him to miss nearly
half a year's work in 1908 and in January 1909, he was
given sick leave from his job with the Land Commission.
He went back to Kerry and did not return to his job
until 1913. He probably finished *The Pie-Dish* and *The
Dandy Dolls* in 1908 while free from his job. The
former play was produced at the Abbey in 1908, but
The Dandy Dolls was rejected and not performed at all
until Austin Clarke's Lyric Theatre Company did it in
1945. I have already suggested that *The Pie-Dish* did not
fulfill the critics' expectations for comedy. *The Dandy
Dolls* was more of the same and the Abbey wanted no
part of it. On his long sick leave, Fitzmaurice wrote *The*

Moonlighter and *The Magic Glasses. The Moonlighter,* a full-length tragedy and one of Fitzmaurice's best plays, would remain unperformed until 1948.

In 1912 the Abbey Theatre revived *The Country Dressmaker,* as it would continue to do until 1949. Fitzmaurice's play was the first full-length Abbey play to be revived. In 1913 the Abbey produced *The Magic Glasses* and once again the response of the Dublin critics was negative. Fitzmaurice, they said, has no business writing comedy in which the hero dies. Fitzmaurice, of course, always preferred reality to the narrow aesthetic legalism of the critics. *Five Plays* was published by Maunsel in Dublin in 1914 and by Little, Brown in Boston in 1917. The book contained the three plays which had been performed at the Abbey, *The Country Dressmaker, The Pie-Dish, The Magic Glasses,* as well as two other plays, *The Moonlighter* and *The Dandy Dolls.* Thus, on the eve of the Easter Rising, George Fitzmaurice's plays were known to Irish audiences.

Things changed after World War I. Fitzmaurice served with the British army in France, "Kitchener's Army." No records have been found about his service. Presumably he managed to preserve his characteristic detachment and good humor in the trenches even without his pints of Guinness. When he returned in 1919, he wrote a comedy, *'Twixt the Giltinans and the Carmodys,* which the Abbey performed in 1923. This would be the last Abbey play produced in his lifetime. In 1969, the Abbey finally got around to staging *The Dandy Dolls,* the play which Fitzmaurice considered his best.

In 1924, Fitzmaurice began what would be a long association with Seumas O'Sullivan's *Dublin Magazine.*

Frustrated in his efforts to get his folk-plays produced, he decided to publish them. Between 1924 and 1957, eight Fitzmaurice plays appeared in the magazine: *The Linnaun Shee* (1924), *The Green Stone* (1926), *'Twixt the Giltinans and the Carmodys* (1943), *There are Tragedies and Tragedies* (1948), *One Evening Gleam* (1949), *The Coming of Ewn Andzale* (1954), *The Terrible Baisht* (1954), *The Enchanted Land* (1957). An entire issue of the *Dublin Magazine* was devoted to *The Enchanted Land.* These plays reflect the range of George Fitzmaurice's work, including comedy, tragedy, farce, realistic plays, and folk-plays. The two folk-plays, *The Linnaun Shee* and *The Green Stone,* are intense depictions of the encounter between the human and the nonhuman worlds. *One Evening Gleam* and *The Coming of Ewn Andzale* were probably the last plays Fitzmaurice wrote. Set in Dublin rather than in Kerry, these two plays give sad witness to the tedious quality of life which has lost the visionary gleam.

Professor Slaughter maintains that Fitzmaurice wrote no plays in the decade between 1930 and 1940. He does not, unfortunately, make it clear how he arrived at this judgment. There were four unpublished plays in Fitzmaurice's suitcase when he died, *The Toothache, King of the Barna Men, The Waves of the Sea,* and *The Simple Hanrahans.* Slaughter says that Fitzmaurice wrote the first two before *The Country Dressmaker* and I tend to agree with him. The last two plays, however, are difficult to date from existing records. Fitzmaurice may well have had them around for a long time. Neither of the plays matches the quality of Fitzmaurice's published work.

When Fitzmaurice retired from the civil service at age 65 in 1942, he was completely unknown in the theater. It had been twenty years since any new play of his had been produced in Dublin. But Fitzmaurice's reputation improved after World War II when Austin Clarke and Liam Miller "rediscovered" his plays. Having received Fitzmaurice's permission, Clarke's Lyric Theatre Company produced *The Dandy Dolls* in 1945 and revived *The Magic Glasses* in 1946. It also staged the first production of *The Linnaun Shee* in 1949. Liam Miller saw this revival of *The Magic Glasses* and was prompted to do some research on this "unknown" playwright. He managed to find a copy of *Five Plays* in a Dublin bookshop and became fascinated with *The Moonlighter,* Fitzmaurice's four-act tragedy which had still not been produced some thirty years after its publication. After his own production of *The Magic Glasses,* Miller undertook *The Moonlighter,* which opened at the Peacock Theatre in Dublin in 1948. Miller, who insists that the play's proper title is *The Moonlighters,* notes that "the production of *The Moonlighters* was enthusiastically recieved, with expressions of amazement from the Dublin critics that this fine play had taken so long to reach the stage." In 1952, he produced *One Evening Gleam* for the first time. Only one other Fitzmaurice play was premiered in the dramatist's lifetime and this was *There are Tragedies and Tragedies,* done by the St. Mary's College Musical and Dramatic Society in Dublin in 1953. Fitzmaurice was 76 years old.

George Fitzmaurice died in Dublin on May 12, 1963, at the age of 86. Michael O'hAodha recalls that his funeral from St. Peter's Aungier Street to Mt. Jerome cemetery "was the smallest ever." "George had kept to himself to the last." Liam Miller plans to erect the cornerstone from Bedford House over his grave. Fitzmaurice would have liked this gesture which will put him forever in touch with his beloved North Kerry.

The words of two distinguished Irish writers may bring us closer to George Fitzmaurice the man. Maurice Kennedy describes the Fitzmaurice he met with Liam Miller in 1946.

> A merry little man, you might say: a man who carries his years lightly and seems to have little liking for the veneer, the surface glitter of civilisation, for cinemas and lounge bars. But in his favourite position with his elbows on the counter of a pub and a glass of stout in his free hand, he will talk entertainingly of a variety of matters—of the noble hooded cloaks handed down from generation to generation in Valentia and Bandon, of fairs and funerals in Killorglin and Abbeyfeale, of the decline of the "visiting houses" and the old way of life in his native Kerry, and of the great days of the old time music hall.

Bryan MacMahon, a Kerryman himself, produced his little story for the Abbey production of *The Dandy Dolls* in 1969. It captures precisely the qualities about Fitzmaurice which, as I shall suggest in the following chapter, inspired his most imaginative and convincing plays.

> Many years ago an old rabbit-trapper said to me: "I was ferretin' in Duagh when the duck lid up on me. 'Bad luck to you,' says I with my ear to the burrow, 'you'll keep me here till morning.'
> "I heard a voice comin' from under the ground. It was tellin' of kings and queens, of moonlighters, quack doctors, of pookas and chariots ridin' the night sky.
> "'I'm bewitched,' I told myself. I peeped through the bushes an' I seen Parson Fitzmaurice's son George struttin' up and down the field and he manufacturin' drama."

2

"Wicked Old Children": Fitzmaurice's Folk-plays

In his introduction to *The Plays of George Fitzmaurice: Dramatic Fantasies,* Austin Clarke recalls that during his first meeting with Fitzmaurice the elderly dramatist spoke of the characters in his plays as "wicked old children." In Fitzmaurice's folk-plays, *The Pie-Dish, The Magic Glasses, The Dandy Dolls, The Linnaun Shee,* and *The Green Stone,* the phrase is marvelously appropriate. There is wickedness in the conflict between good and evil, or, more typically, between social values and personal values, between ordinary reality and the dream. All of these plays have "wicked" men in them whose dreams threaten the status quo. But wickedness in the plays goes deeper than this. Unlike most of the characters in his plays. Fitzmaurice is always sympathetic with his visionaries and dreamers. For him the real wickedness of society is its complacency and self-satisfaction. The ambiguity continues in the phrase "old children." In one sense, the societies which Fitzmaurice creates in the plays have never developed an emotional and intellectual maturity to match their biological growth. They are acquisitive, self-seeking, intolerant, violent, and unimaginative. In a deeper sense, however, Fitzmaurice's heroes in these plays are "old children" who have seen visions and dreamed dreams, who are in touch with an order of existence which transcends the ordinary world. These visionaries bring the "old" world, the world of myth, the world of fairy, into the humdrum lives of their families and societies. They are, to quote Bryan MacMahon, truly "children of the rainbow." One of the old men in MacMahon's novel reflects on such a time of connection: "The time I speak of, our lives were so thronged with small beauties that you wouldn't think 'twas sons an' daughters of the flesh we were, but children of the rainbow dwellin' always in the mornin' of the world!"

The term "folk-play" is as ambiguous as "wicked old children." In a sense all of Fitzmaurice's plays, with the exception of *The Coming of Ewn Andzale,* are folk-plays, because they are about Irish countrymen and are written in dialect. Such a broad definition of a critical term, however, limits its usefulness. Even exuberant dramatic experiments like *The Enchanted Land* could be called folk-plays in this broad sense. I have decided, therefore, to label folk-plays only those works which possess certain qualities which other Fitzmaurice plays, though admittedly about rural Ireland, do not have. Chief among these would be the presence of the fairy world or the mythic world in the real world of the play. This presence can take the form of an actual intrusion of supernatural forces, as is the case in several of the plays, or it can be the effect of a previous contact with the supernatural on the life of a character, as in *The Pie-Dish.* Another quality of the folk-play would be lyricism, a poetic-prose through which the visionary tries to communicate his experience to those around him. A third quality would be sympathy. When Fitzmaurice writes comedies like *The Country Dressmaker, 'Twixt the Giltinans and the Carmodys,* or *The Simple Hanrahans,* we sympathize with no one. All the characters have limited vision. But in his folk-plays, Fitzmaurice clearly identifies with his sensitive and imaginative heroes and he expects us to do likewise.

Two other qualities of Fitzmaurice's folk-plays need to be distinguished, namely, grotesquerie and violence. I have included these qualities last because one of them, grotesquerie, is not present in all of the folk-plays, and the other, violence, is present in plays other than folk-plays. But the kind of violence which occurs in the interface between the real world and the world of spirits is a very special violence indeed, more intense and more destructive than that in other plays. These then are the qualities which define Fitzmaurice's folk-plays: supernaturalism, lyricism, sympathy, grotesquerie, and violence.

My distinction of Fitzmaurice's plays as folk-plays, realistic plays, and dramatic experiments does not always conform to the Dolmen Press Edition's distinction of the plays. The editors there give no explanation of why the plays were divided into what they call folk-plays, realistic plays, and dramatic fantasies. Most of what Austin Clarke has called dramatic fantasies I have included in the present chapter as folk-plays. And I question Howard Slaughter's use of the term "folk-play" for plays as different as *The King of the Barna Men, The Pie-Dish,* and *The Moonlighter.*

The first of Fitzmaurice's folk-plays, *The Pie-Dish,*

was produced at the Abbey Theatre in March, 1908, during the same theatrical season as *The Country Dressmaker,* which had appeared the previous October. Several of the Abbey's leading players, including Sara Allgood, Arthur Sinclair, and J. M. Kerrigan, were in the cast as they had been in the earlier play. The play had a total of twenty-three performances at the Abbey between 1908 and 1912 and it was taken on three Abbey tours to England in the same period.

Leum Donoghue, the central character in *The Pie-Dish,* is the first of Fitzmaurice's "madmen," a category which would later include Jaymony Shanahan in *The Magic Glasses,* Roger Carmody in *The Dandy Dolls,* Jamesie Kennelley in *The Linnaun Shee,* and Martineen Collopy in *The Green Stone.* Each of these men is obsessed with the spirit world and speaks and acts in ways bewildering to those around him. Leum Donoghue, once a reliable tradesman and father, now over eighty years old, has for twenty years been obsessed with making a pie dish. He has never been able to finish the job, but is convinced he will complete it before he dies.

The play is about Leum's last hour of life. It opens with his two grandsons, Jack and Eugene, discussing his obsession and the debilitating effect this has on their mother, Margaret, who is Leum's daughter. We learn that Leum has been having raving fits and Margaret enters to ask one of the boys to go for the priest. At this point, Johanna, another daughter, arrives to berate her sister for the poor care being taken of their father. Johanna, however, is in no position to criticize, having forced Leum out of her own house some twenty years earlier. One thinks of Lear and filial ingratitude. The

priest arrives just about the time Leum awakens and prepares to give him the last rites. Leum will have none of this, however, claiming he can't die because his pie-dish lies unfinished.

Leum's obsession, it seems, stems from the time, twenty years earlier, when he was moving from Johanna to Margaret and spent the night asleep in an old fort — very likely one of the numerous promontory forts which cling to coastal cliffs in Kerry. From then on the old man would have nothing but the pie-dish. The priest interprets this obsession as the work of the devil and attempts to persuade Leum from his sinful ways. Leum, however, feeling his life ebbing from him, finally implores the devil for time to finish his pie-dish. He dies blaspheming and the priest concludes that he is damned. Daughter Margaret is less certain about what happens beyond the grave. All she knows, she says, is that her father is dead.

It should first of all be noted for readers unfamiliar with Irish usage that the pie-dish in the title is more like what we would call a stew-pot, a deep-welled vessel for making meat-pies. All in all an odd vehicle for such heavy symbolism. But I suppose what the pie-dish shares with the other talismans Fitzmaurice uses in his folk-plays — glasses, dolls, a stone — is commonness. The dramatist is telling us that the extraordinary is right there in the ordinary, if one only looks hard enough. He knows that the gods always operate through the simplest elements, earth, air, fire, and water.

The pie-dish, then, is a normally utilitarian object which Leum Donoghue treats as a potentially perfect work of art. He can never get it finished, though, because it exists ideally only in his imagination. A man with an abnormal dread of death, Leum believes that obsessive creativity guarantees earthly immortality. In his own mind at least, this concern had done the trick for the past twenty years, so why not for twenty more.

Fitzmaurice uses supernaturalism in this play more indirectly than he will use it in later plays. Grotesque creatures do not appear on stage; the talisman never produces any magical effects. All of this is just hinted at, as if Fitzmaurice were trying something out on his audience to test its sympathetic response. And *The Pie-Dish* had a respectable run at the Abbey and on tour, despite the fact that reviewers didn't like what they called Fitzmaurice's blending of comedy and tragedy. The later folk-plays would be more explicit, more fantastical, truer, I think, to Fitzmaurice's own imagination. But he would have great difficulty getting these plays produced and would finally despair of the theater entirely.

To return to the play: Leum's death brings to an intense climax the conflict between Christianity and paganism, which will be a favorite theme for Fitzmaurice in all of his folk-plays. Does the traditional "God bless" have any efficacy in a world of alien and mysterious powers? Does man have any control over his fate? Father Troy, spokesman for the most dogmatic and complacent kind of Christianity, tries to force Leum into an Act of Contrition. Leum will have no part of it, yet cannot "go gentle into that good night." He dies of nothing but a rage to live.

LEUM God above, isn't it time I will get after all? Ah, 'tis killing me that pain is. Good God in heaven, it's time I must get—if it isn't time from God I'll get, maybe the devil will give me time! Let the devil himself give me time, then, let him give me time to finish my pie-dish, and it's his I'll be for ever more, body and soul! *[He shakes. The pie-dish falls and breaks. He screams and falls back on chair.]* (II,56)

Leum's unrepentant blasphemy makes an extraordinary ending for an Irish play—and indeed Joseph Holloway and others thought the play a bit of a scandal.

Yet this unusual ending of *The Pie-Dish* has a complex meaning. Fitzmaurice is not simply coming out against a complacent and uncharitable clergy, though he has no use for priests in his plays. He is questioning the whole idea of human power. A priest can have no certain knowledge of Leum's fate, as Margaret reminds Father Troy. "But it isn't certain entirely that it is damned he is, Father Troy? . . . 'Tisn't damned he is, and no sin on him but what he did in the heel. But it's dead he is . . . May the Lord have mercy on his soul!" (II,56) Like the priest, Leum has convinced himself that he possesses special powers, but ultimately he cannot control his own death. In other folk-plays, Fitzmaurice will dramatize a more proper human response than Leum Donoghue's to the authentic and mysterious powers in the world, a humbler, more accepting, more patient attitude in which one does not seek to control, but merely to experience these powers.

Leum Donoghue's desperate final scream underscores a violence which is present throughout the play and very common indeed in the worlds of Fitzmaurice's plays. Anger and violence, he seems to be saying, are present in normal human relations and dramatize the failure of

human communication. One is hard put to find an expression of love in these plays, except for the love of the
dreamer for his dream. And perhaps that is the only
experience of love Fitzmaurice himself ever had. *The
Pie-Dish* begins with a report of Margaret's screech as
Leum enters his death-throes. Eugene declares that if his
grandfather is moved into the upstairs room "he'd kick
the traces and go wild all out if he woke up and found
himself there." (II, 44) Margaret speaks of her father as
"prancing about the floor with the eyes lepping out of
his head." (II, 46) Johanna wants to take the pie-dish
and "smash it into smithereens." (II, 49) Leum reacts to
being moved with an almost Lear-like frenzy. "Will you
houl', you thing! . . . Let me go—go from me—or it's to
scrope those two smooth cheeks I will with these nails
and claw the two eyes out of your yellow head!" (II,
51) and Eugene threatens the meddling Johanna with
his grandfather nodding approval.

> EUGENE *[limping after* JOHANNA] Leave go of him,
> Joan Bawn, or it's to ram the tongs I will down your mortal
> throat. *[drags* JOHANNA *off* LEUM]
> LEUM Good man, Eugene! Beat her, slash her, and stamp
> on her carcass! (II, 51)

Fitzmaurice's next folk-play, *The Magic Glasses,* was
accepted by the Abbey Theatre and produced by Lennox Robinson in April and October, 1913. It closed
after a short run and was not again performed by the
Abbey until a revival in 1967. Austin Clarke and Liam
Miller both produced the play shortly after World War
II, as has been indicated earlier. *The Magic Glasses* was
the last Fitzmaurice play the Abbey Theatre would do
until 1923.

The play concerns the precariousness of civilization in the face of the powers of man and of the fairies. Padden Shanahan and his wife Maineen are the parents of a thirty-eight-year-old son, Jaymony, who has for some time before the play opens taken to spending his time in the loft of the house rather than fulfilling his parents's social expectations. Refusing either to work or to marry, Jaymony prefers to contemplate what he calls the "Magic Glasses" he once purchased at a fair. Padden and Maineen, puzzled by this extraordinary behavior, request the services of a local quack, Morgan Quille, who has built a reputation for "curing" ailments of all kinds. Quille arrives, coaxes Jaymony from his perch, questions him about his symptoms, prescribes an incredible cure and leaves. The "cure" seems to work for a short time, but then Jaymony escapes again to the loft, this time for good. The play concludes with a Wagnerian flourish, as Jaymony's loft disappears in an explosion and Jaymony is found dangling and dead, his throat slit by the magic glasses. The heretofore bewildered family has no trouble coping with a corpse and their keening announces the return of customary social ritual as the curtain falls.

The focus in *The Magic Glasses* is on civilization, which is threatened on the one hand by human will and on the other by the spirit world. Morgan Quille suggests both of these threatening forces. No one in the community knows for sure whether Quille cures by potions or by punches. We hear early on in the play that he has cured Mary Canty of the dropsies, Looney Carroll of madness, and Josie Pratt of a mouth disorder. But Padden and his wife are uncertain about whether the cures came from Quille's "dilution of the white heather" and "blue lozenge," or whether he simply terrified his poor patients into health.

> PADDEN ... another man was eyewitness to the way he managed Looney Carroll, chasing him through a wood in the dead hour of the night till the fool ran up again a tree unbeknownst, was flung back on his back, the blood of a pig spouting out of his nostrils, and, signs by, the fool won't go around a tree since. (I, 4)

Padden describes Morgan Quille as "a man, ... a strange man, and he rising like a cloud over the gap in Peg Caxty's bounds ditch," and later comments, "he's the biggest and the blackest man I ever seen." (I, 5) We know Quille is a charlatan, but he nevertheless has about him the power of black magic.

The central conflict in the play involves Quille and Jaymony. We first believe Jaymony to be a lazy ne'er-do-well who has lived off his parents to the ripe old age of thirty-eight. When Jaymony, who is not present for the first third of the play, finally climbs down from the loft, his language has the hollow bravura of a Captain Boyle.

> JAYMONY I'm warning you if the tea isn't drawn the minute I hop down out of this, there isn't a mug in the dresser I won't smash, and I'll break the window, and so every divil around the house will make it the sorry day to you you got into the habit of renayging me in the tea. (I, 10)

But, as is usual in a Fitzmaurice play, the situation is more complex than this. During the examination by Quille, we learn that Jaymony is a romantic idealist who has rejected the drab cacaphony of his parents' world and, thanks to the magical powers of the glasses, can escape from the humdrum into the world of fairy. When Quille asks him why he spends his time in the loft, Jaymony replies, "'tis better than being in the slush—same old thing every day—this an ugly spot, and the people ugly, grumpy, and savage." (I, 11)

Jaymony's description of his purchase of the magic glasses possesses a lyrical beauty that reminds me of Synge. "It's through a wood the brown woman came to me, and it wasn't a crackle or a noise at all she made and she walking on the grass so green. She stood for a while where the bluebells grow." (I, 11-12) The "brown woman" sells Jaymony a set of nine magic glasses, three brown, three red, and three blue. The owner of such magic glasses can enter another world where drab realities drop away and he can fulfill his most secret wishes. The perception of fantasy is, of course, limited by the quality of one's imagination and Jaymony is no Yeats. Rather than gaining aesthetic satisfaction, Jaymony fulfills his desire for power in the possession of riches (the brown glasses), women (the red glasses), and reknown (the blue glasses). Harry Clarke has captured Jaymony's fantasy with the magic glasses perfectly in the portion of his "Geneva Window" devoted to Fitzmaurice's play. The window now belongs to the Municipal Gallery of Modern Art, Dublin.

The character of Morgan Quille is as ambiguous as that of Jaymony. Quille first impresses us as a typical quack and the situation seems purely comic. He addresses Jaymony in a macaronic patois hardly likely to exorcize any devils!

QUILLE Down on your knees now, you haunted thing. Keep looking at me or I'll send this red-hot tongs fizzling

down into your baistly guts. Sacramento, Dominus vobis-
cum, mea culpa, mea maxima culpa, kyrie eleison, excel-
sior! I abjure thee by these words, tell me what you are and
what you aren't. (I, 10)

And yet after Jaymony delivers an oracular message
about the power of the glasses, Quille is seized with
convulsions and is barely able to gasp out a remedy of
wine, hops on one leg, fourteen red roses, and shovels of
red earth, before he is propelled out the door crying
"my time is limited, my time is limited." (I, 14)

Fitzmaurice is clearly suggesting that the supernatural
remains problematic in Kerry. Jaymony's dream vision
and Quille's convulsions can be interpreted as pathologi-
cal and purely naturalistic. But the audience is left won-
dering what has really happened in this house and
whether perhaps there has been one of those apparently
random incursions of the timeless into time which mark
human history.

The power of Christianity itself is problematic here
and in Fitzmaurice's plays generally. Christian refer-
ences fill the play, but mainly as rhetorical common-
places unconnected to faith. Phrases like "Holy Father,"
"Mother of God," "For the love of God" occur with
typically Irish frequency and unreflectiveness. And yet
when Quille persuades Jaymony to go through the Sign
of the Cross with him, power does flow. The symbolic
gesture begins the ritual of exorcism which concludes
with Quille's convulsions and Jaymony's violent death.
Fitzmaurice provides no empirical certainties. Life is
farce and the commonplace, but it is also ritual and
myth.

Like *The Magic Glasses, The Dandy Dolls* is a play

about the intrusion of supernatural powers into the fragile civilization of a Kerry home. And again it is the fairies who prevail over the expostulations and rituals of Christianity. Violence and fear lie just beneath the surface of the farcical blather. Roger Carmody makes dandy dolls, and the action of the play concerns various intrigues to get his latest model — a perfect example of the species — away from him. Fitzmaurice characteristically refuses to be specific about the nature of the dolls, except to suggest that they, like the magic glasses, provide an entree into the world of imagination and art. Roger at one point makes a scathing comparison between his wife Cauth's aging — "Cauth of the ugly snout," he calls her — and the timeless beauty of the dolls.

Cauth Carmody has little sympathy for her husband's preoccupation with dollmaking. She is one of the practical people, like Padden and Maineen in *The Magic Glasses,* interested only in keeping food on the table and clothes on the children. She has no deeper needs than these and she asks no deeper questions. She has no understanding of her husband's curse or blessing, but knows simply that it frustrates her housekeeping.

The play begins as a mysterious character identified only as the Grey Man appears at the home of Roger and Cauth Carmody to inquire about the dandy dolls. Like Morgan Quille in *The Magic Glasses,* the Grey Man brings a threatening presence into the apparently defenseless territory of the Carmody's home.

> CAUTH Such jokes don't match your beard, old fairy, or whatever you are, and wherever you rose out of this haunted eve of May. (I,24)

We hear from the Grey Man of another enigmatic creature, The Hag's Son, who has a fondness for perfectly made dandy dolls and has spirited away all such models that Roger has made. Here is another creature from Fitzmaurice's fantasy, a creature both attractive and repulsive, a kind of Caliban restored to power:

> GREY MAN Calling for his prizes he does be, the little blackguard brat, screeching, laughing, and he turning every somersault for himself on the slippery green above.... He has old Mohoon totally off his stems, his white head up day and night with fury going through his beard like a whirlwind through a bush. (I,26)

Father James, the local pastor, joins the Grey Man, the Hag, and the Hag's Son in pursuit of the dandy dolls. Coming ostensibly to admonish Carmody for stealing his geese, Father James seizes the doll and quickly baptizes it to put it under his power! "So be it, then, and Jug shall be her name.... There, now; she's sanctified and sacramental sound, a match for all the hags and hags' sons from Barna to Kanturk. In holy armour, therefore, she's ready for the fray." (I,33)

The climax of the play cannot really be called a battle for the dandy doll. Neither the priest nor the Grey Man has powers equal to those of the Hag and her Son. These latter two arrive and reenact the ritual theft of the doll. Roger dimly senses that he is in the presence of inexorable forces when he cries, "He has it! Lord, he has it! Sure he had to have it, and where's the good in talking, and all to no use, for it's fore-doomed I was, it's fore-doomed I was." (I,36) His wife Cauth expresses the same sentiments with much lievelier imagery and rhythm: " ... them dolls the biggest torment to him in the world. For the Hag's Son is against them to the death, and so sure as Roger makes a doll, so sure will the Hag's Son, soon or late, come at it, give it a knuckle in the navel, split it in two fair halves, collar the windpipe, and off with him carrying the squeaky-squeak." (I,22)

This time, however, possession of the dandy doll is not enough and the strange creatures take Roger himself with them.

> KEERBY ... didn't I see Roger being carried away by the Hag and the Son of the Hag. Riding on two Spanish asses they were, holding him between them by a whisker each, and his whiskers were the length of six feet you'd think, and his nose was the length of six feet you'd think, and his eyes were the size of turnips bulging outside his head. Galloping like the wind they were, through the pass of the Barna mountains, sweeping him along with them, for ever and ever, to their woeful den in the heart of the Barna hills. (I, 37)

The play ends at this point with no one quite sure what has happened or why, except that supernatural powers have once again been demonstrated to the country people.

The Linnaun Shee, like *The Magic Glasses* and *The Dandy Dolls,* is a play about the interpenetration of reality and fantasy. It was produced by the Lyric Theatre company at the Abbey Theatre in 1949. The play's hero, Jamesie Kennelly, like Jaymony Shanahan and Roger Carmody, has access to a world radically different from the normal domestic and business world. The link between these two levels of experience is the Linnaun Shee, a shape-shifting female whom some men see as a withered croaking hag and others as the fairest of the fair. Her name, Professor Slaughter tells us, means "phantom lover." Like the Pied Piper, she lures men away from hearth and house with her song and leads them to a mysterious fate in the hills.

Fitzmaurice seems preoccupied with this possibility of escape from the humdrum, the isolation, the insensitivity, the violence, and the pretentiousness of North Kerry domestic life. Imagination and fantasy exist for him as a means of entering a more perfect world. One can easily see Fitzmaurice himself as the central figure in *The Magic Glasses, The Dandy Dolls,* and *The Linnaun Shee.* His work as a civil servant must have seemed incredibly dull to a romantic dreamer. How perfectly fine it would have been to meet up with the Linnaun Shee on one of his walks down Baggott Street and to be whisked off to the land of his heart's desire.

The play deals with the disruption of a respectable Kerry household by a mysterious power which turns out to be the Linnaun Shee. Hanora Kennelly, who normally confides in her friends Julia and Mary, is being very tight-lipped about what ails her husband, Jamesie. Almost half the play deals with the reactions of several characters to Hanora's uncharacteristic taciturnity. When she finally comes on stage, Hanora reveals the cause of her anxiety, the fear that her fifty-five-year-old husband will be spirited away by the Linnaun Shee just as he almost was in the days before their marriage.

Daniel Tobin, a relative and "the best farmer in the County Kerry" arrives for some business dealings with Jamesie only to find him raving about "my lovely one, my lovely one" whose arrival is imminent. Despite Tobin's scepticism, a character does arrive whom the others experience as a withered hag, but whom Jamesie experiences as the lady of his dreams. Yielding readily to her beckonings, Jamesie leaves the house and is seen by the others being lured across the quarry water "black and deep and cold" to the hills beyond. There Daniel Tobin witnesses a transformation which challenges his middle-class smugness.

> DANIEL Faith, I'm seeing something teetotally differ-ent . . . but, faith, it's no longer Jamesie Kennelly is with her, but my young buck of a Timothy Dansell, the man that's contracted to marry my daughter Johann come next Shrove itself. . . . My hand to you, it's no longer yellow or withered she is, and she having herself back into the form of her youth — the form the old people used to know her by. I suppose she is as purty as Jamesie says, but what wonder is that and she setting up to be some sort of fairy queen? (I,53)

Unlike Roger Carmody in *The Dandy Dolls,* however, Jamesie does not remain in the enchanted land. Something, we are not certain what — though it may have been an antidote provided by one of Hanora's rela-tives — conteracts the magic and restores Jamesie to his family and his farm at the play's end.

Fitzmaurice's intention in the play becomes quite clear in this reunion scene. Jamesie, hitherto absorbed in the pleasures of the imagination, is now stripped of this visionary gleam and restored to the dull consciousness of a country farmer. Looking "queer and haggard," Jamesie appears at the door of his house and immedi-ately his thoughts turn to business:

> JAMESIE Alluding to that brindled heifer, let Jacksen be going to bed early for himself so he'll be up with the first light in the morning to help me to take her to the Big Fair — and we can't be too early, likewise, if we don't want

to lose money in the price, and the Dublin buyers arriving in Abbeyfeale tonight. (I,54)

The same thing will happen to Eugene Guerin in *The Moonlighter.*

The Linnaun Shee is at once a more experimental and a less successful play than either *The Magic Glasses* or *The Dandy Dolls.* Fitzmaurice is trying to rationalize his fantasy and to make more conventional his scenes of domestic life. I suspect he was disappointed that *The Dandy Dolls* was not produced and was trying for a formula which would make his basic themes more attractive and comprehensible in the commercial theater. The effort was fruitless, however. *The Linnaun Shee* was not performed until twenty-five years after its appearance in the *Dublin Magazine* in 1924.

With regard to elements of fantasy in *The Linnaun Shee,* Fitzmaurice has replaced the ambiguous, violent, and hieratic powers in *The Magic Glasses* and *The Dandy Dolls* with the transparent symbolism of the Lady who brings the dreamer to the fulfillment of his dream. Even the intruder's language has been regularized. Compare the following lines from *The Dandy Dolls* with lines from *The Linnaun Shee:*

HAG'S SON *[laughing shrilly]* A spit for his baptizing, for my old mother, the Hag, took the virtue out of it, and she, the minute he shook the holy water, giving me a puff of her breath in between the two eyes that blew me in a balloon right over the highest peak of the Barna hills. *(Dandy Dolls,* I, 35)

THE HAG *[taking flute from mouth]* Ha-ha! is it flamming my little boy they are? *[hits* CAUTH *with flute]* Take that, old snotty nose! go wash your rotten rags and grease your creaking bones!

CAUTH I'm kilt.

THE HAG *[hitting priest]* Ha-ha, shiny green coat, I have slaughtered a flay on the nape of your neck! *[hits him again]* Take that on the small of your back and scratch yourself!

FATHER JAMES *[itching himself]* Botheration! In the name of the Father!

THE HAG *[to her son]* Fight away, my gamey boy! fight away, my hearty. Your mother is up to your ear *[singing]* and we'll rise a grand song and we'll rise a grand tune, going back to our home in Barna. *(Dandy Dolls,* I, 36)

LINNAUN SHEE   Come away, come along, come away —
Come, and we'll go roaming;
Fast by the winding Feale we'll rove
And by Poul Tharriv's foaming.
In Donal's fort we'll spend a while,
When the moon is brightly shining,
In Glounamucmae we'll stay till day
And we won't be repining.

(Linnaun Shee, I, 52)

The lines from *The Linnaun Shee* lack the richness of diction and rhythm which occur often in the earlier play.

Fitzmaurice was obviously capable in his best plays of a dramatic language as evocative as that of Synge. Irving Wardle has described Fitzmaurice's North Kerry dialect as "a knobbly, irregular speech, full of half-assimilated alien expressions, submerged proverbs, quirkish word order and natural imagery." He could just as well have been writing about Synge. Indeed it has been said that, at its best, Fitzmaurice's dramatic idiom was closer to the actual speech of the West than Synge's because the latter was always concerned with shaping the language of his characters into art. But in *The Linnaun Shee* Fitzmaurice substitutes convention for creativity and the result is unfortunate.

Not only the language, but the characterization is less interesting in *The Linnaun Shee* than it is in *The Magic Glasses* and *The Dandy Dolls.* Sharp-tongued Cauth Carmody in *The Dandy Dolls* is here the long-suffering Hanora Kennelly. Hanora is socially adjusted with "her fine baan of cows, a son going to be a priest, another going to be a doctor; a lady of a daughter will likely be a nun, and good childre at home; money in the bank, avico." (I,43-44) Her character and those of Daniel Tobin and the servants belong more to the problem plays of Ibsen and Chekov than to the Irish folk experience. Even Jamesie mouths banalities when he describes his "queen of loveliness." "But how could I describe to you the aspects of my Queen of Loveliness that it has failed them all to describe — all the poets since the world began? 'Tisn't to be described they could be, and the snowdrop no compare to the sheen of her whiteness, the reddest and loveliest rose nothing to the blush she sometimes wore." (I,50) Nothing in this language persuades us that it could be spoken by a real person with real feelings. In their moments of greatest intensity the visionaries in both *The Magic Glasses* and *The Dandy Dolls* use "real talk" and it works well.

The Green Stone, the last of George Fitzmaurice's folk-plays, is a minor one-act play, never performed, but published in *The Dublin Magazine* in 1926. It concerns yet another middle-aged Irish dreamer who possesses a talisman. A minor work, it nevertheless deals with themes which are common to all of Fitzmaurice's folk-plays: the microcosm of North Kerry, the value of personal freedom, the tedium of a social routine determined by acquisitiveness, the source of personal fulfillment in nature, and the implicit loneliness of every honest man's journey on the earth. The plays are about simple people whose lives can now and again be touched by magic to make them for a time children of the rainbow.

3

"Anything But A Loveable Lot": Fitzmaurice's Realistic Plays

The plays considered in this chapter cannot be so easily categorized as the "folk-plays" of the last chapter which shared a common ground of supernaturalism, lyricism, and sympathy. In these folk-plays human action is controlled by powers beyond ordinary reality and an "other world" often intrudes into "this world." The relation of the most sensitive and sympathetic characters in these folk-plays to the "other world" is both romantic and tragic, and a longing for the impossible dream expresses itself in moving lyrical passages. The plays which I have grouped under the heading "realistic plays" do not have this element of supernaturalism about them, with human action being controlled by alien forces. They deal rather with human willfulness and its consequences.

All of the realistic plays are "folk" plays in the broad

sense because they are about the experience of common people and mainly country people, though two of the plays, *One Evening Gleam* and *The Coming of Ewn Andzale,* are set in Dublin. Several of the plays are comedies, including Fitzmaurice's best-known play, *The Country Dressmaker.* His other comedies, *'Twixt the Giltinans and the Carmodys, The Simple Hanrahans, The Terrible Baisht,* and *There are Tragedies and Tragedies,* resemble *The Country Dressmaker* in theme and form, though none of the later comedies matches its quality. *The Coming of Ewn Andzale,* also a comedy and Fitzmaurice's last play, has a broader significance than any of the other comedies, though it is not as skillfully constructed. *The Moonlighter* and *One Evening Gleam* are tragedies, the first a four-act play dealing with the impact of Irish nationalism on several Kerry families; the second, set in a Dublin tenement and possibly based on Fitzmaurice's personal experience, a one-act tragedy of alienation which reveals the dullness of city-dwellers for whom the dream has become a symptom of neurosis.

I want to begin with *The Moonlighter,* one of Fitzmaurice's best plays, because it contains elements of both the folk-play and the realistic play, and thus has connections with the works I have discussed in chapter 2 and chapter 3. Written very early in Fitzmaurice's career, *The Moonlighter* was published in *Five Plays* (1914), though not performed for more than thirty years. (Liam Miller produced the play at the Peacock Theatre in 1948.)

The Moonlighter chronicles the fortunes of the Guerin, Driscoll, and Carmody families in the period just after the turn of the century and before the Rising of 1916. Peter Guerin, a successful dairy farmer in Kerry, has little sympathy for the nationalistic senti-ments of his sons. So strongly opposed is he to such ideology that he sends his radical sons packing off across the sea rather than have them consumed by patriotism. Guerin himself is identified with the enemies of nation-alism, and thus with another ideology which would keep the landowners and rentgrabbers in power. The tragedy of *The Moonlighter* is especially Peter Guerin's tragedy, as he discovers that both ideologies encourage the human violence which finally claims his own life.

The play opens with the sardonic matchmaker Ma-lachi Cantillon attempting to make a match between Luke Carmody's daughter Breeda and Peter Guerin's only remaining son, Eugene. We learn, however, that Malachi's efforts may prove futile, since there are al-ready romantic bonds between Eugene and Maura Dris-coll and between Breeda and Tom Driscoll. But old Luke Carmody sees a better profit in a match between his daughter and Eugene Guerin.

Peter Guerin arrives, furious at the news that his last son too has shown signs of becoming a nationalist. Eugene admits that he wants to become a moonlighter, one of a group of militant nationalists who operate at night. But his motives are romantic rather than political and he sees this as a way of pursuing his vision of the Dark Rosaleen. We are immediately fearful for his wel-fare in a society which encourages opportunists like Luke Carmody and Malachi Cantillon. Tom Driscoll, also a moonlighter, is much more politically motivated than his friend Eugene.

Act II begins with Malachi and Ellen Guerin, Eugene's mother, hiding in a glen late at night to spy on the moonlighters. Eugene appears with Tom Driscoll and is sworn in to membership by Captain Synan. Plans are made for a raid on the local Great House, a symbol of the oppressive landlord in every Irish town, and for other moves against expropriation of their own lands. In Act III, Malachi is revealed as the real villain of the piece, ready to loan money to large landowners so that they can buy up the smaller lands around them. This sort of activity probably dates the play after the Land Act of 1903, when such speculation in land by native Irish became possible. Malachi is also revealed to be an informer who has tried to thwart the attack on the Great House. During a romantic interlude Tom and Eugene fall asleep in the arms of Breeda and Maura, and they miss their date with the moonlighters, who descend upon the Guerin house to find their comrades. Peter Guerin thus learns for certain that his son is a moonlighter and thus, in his eyes, a traitor. In a moving scene, he throws this "scamp of the world" out of his house and Eugene leaves cursing his father. The act ends with Peter Guerin declaring, "I have done my duty by Eugene." (II, 132)

A year has passed when Act IV begins and the scene is once again Peter Guerin's kitchen. The moonlighters' organization has been broken. Eugene has been gone for the year, but this has made no change in his father's bitterness. Ellen Guerin laments that "flaming years have passed over our heads, and we have brought our scars out of the raging battling times," but hopes that "we'll all rise contented at to-morrow's dawn, calm and

rational for ourselves, without the pains of villainous
torments darting through our eyeballs." (II,135) Her
hopes will not be realized. Word has come from Eugene
that he is finally returning home, but before he arrives
we learn of the various tragedies which have happened
since he left. Maura Driscoll, his intended, has gone mad
because she feels responsible for her brother Tom's fate.
She had told the moonlighters to "take Tom" instead
of Eugene to attack the Great House. Eileen Guerin has
died. Tom Driscoll has become a murderer for the cause,
has been captured, and awaits execution. Eugene arrives
and is a totally changed person. A year of life in the city
has destroyed his romantic idealism and left in its place
self-centeredness and cynicism.

Eugene's mother rejoices in her son's change of heart,
but Peter Guerin listens to his son in silence, reflecting
no doubt on what his act of "duty" toward him has
accomplished. Mad Maura Driscoll appears and, upon
observing Eugene, declares, "They say Eugene came
home. But I can't be deceived. It is an imposter that is
here and not Eugene. They swept him away to a mysterious place, and he'll return no more." (II,145) Eugene
hears the news of his sister's death and observes Maura's
madness with indifference. He has lost his ability to
sympathize. At this point Tom Driscoll bursts in, es-
caped from the gallows, and asks Peter Guerin for a gun.
It is a moment of truth for Peter and the trauma of
seeing his son whose soul he has helped kill together
with the condemned Tom Driscoll shocks him into
going to Tom's aid. Shouting, "The dirty police! Ah, the
dirty police!", Peter Guerin rushes out of the house
with Tom. Both are shot, of course, and all Eugene can
say is,

> Why will you be going on like that, mother? He rushed to his death in a spurt of folly, and who could stop him? Why will you be turning away—in God's name, look at me with the soft look of a mother, for I'm in torment too! . . . Be just to me itself. You didn't expect me to do what father done, surely? The best of his time was spent, but think of what I'd have to lose by facing the police on a forlorn hope, losing all that lay before me—fifty or sixty years maybe of a bounding, vigorous life. (II, 149)

His self-centered indifference contrasts sharply with the others around him, his mother, even the cynical Malachi, and especially Breeda, who has now lost her man and whose lament as the curtain falls bears witness to the meaninglessness of it all and the far distance they all are from the moral wellspring of nature. "Ah, what signifies it now what any one did or didn't, since he is dead? But it is for him and the like of him that the flowers smile, and always smiled, in the green soil of Ireland." (II, 150)

The Moonlighter, despite some obvious melodrama, is a very moving play and it remains one of the mysteries in the history of the Abbey Theatre that *The Country Dressmaker* was chosen for production and *The Moonlighter* was not. One can only assume that the political elements in the play made it risky in the decade before the Rising. In intensity of feeling, in depth of characterization, in lyrical dialect, and in consciousness of the tragedy of life, Fitzmaurice's play compares very well with the best of Synge, Colum, and O'Casey.

The play in its tragic vision has elements of both the folk-play and the realistic play. Like the folk-play, it contains fatalism and resignation, especially on the part of the play's two mothers, Ellen Guerin and Peg Driscoll. What happens is assumed to be the result of inexorable and mysterious forces that control human lives. Pagan and Christian attitudes are blended in their consciousness.

At the same time, like the realistic play, *The Moonlighter* strongly suggests that tragedy is the result of human will, not of supernatural determinism. The actions of men in the play, Malachi, Eugene, Tom, and especially Peter Guerin, are not controlled or predetermined and these people must suffer the consequences of their own actions. For his usury and informing, Malachi must have a lonely old age, **shunned and distrusted by all** around him. Tom has killed a man quite deliberately and is killed in turn. But dying, he is no wiser. Peter's pride reaps for him a bitter harvest in the curse of his own son. His tragedy deepens when his last son returns home a mirror image of his father's values, and Peter Guerin has the terrifying experience of listening to himself. Peter's final brave and loving action, his defense of the doomed Tom Driscoll, comes too late. There is recognition and there is destruction. A tragic pattern indeed.

I have noted above a passage early in the play where Peg Driscoll bewails the fairy presence and its calamitous consequences for those she loves. She and Ellen Guerin are two mothers who feel trapped by forces they do not understand. Ellen's lament sounds a good deal like the old mother in Synge's *Riders to the Sea:*

> ELLEN I am tormented from every abuse of the world, whirled about like an old bruised and battered tin-can. But 'tis for the crimes of more I am punished, Eileen, for it's nothing I ever done out of the way to deserve these stripes uncommon and severe, scarified all my days with troubles walloping at me as fierce as hailstones flamming on the slate. (II, 96)

Peg has "forebodings ... and tokens and dreams" (II, 97) and exclaims, "Rivers of blood I seen going past our door; and it's my son Tom I seen hanging from the gallows, a pale dead corpse I seen him hanging." (II, 98) All of the omens prove true. Morgan Synan, Captain of the Moonlighters, has a premonition of his own death when he hears the cry of the banshee. "My age is twenty-five, but my end is drawing near. There is them has heard the banshee three times and she making for our cabin. Up the banks of the river she do be coming, the voice going in and out with every turn of the river, and it flowing crooked through the green inches." (II, 114)

Although they utter fatalistic sentiments, the women try to maintain their faith in the Christian God. In some way, no matter how dire the premonitions, the purposeful hand of God must be working. In the midst of her recollections of various omens at the opening of *The Moonlighter*, Ellen Guerin declares her faith in God's providence, "a new and special trouble sent to me for some purpose by the Lord God, glory, honour, and praise to be His holy name!" (II, 96)

At the end of the play when the fugitive Tom Driscoll is about to appear, his mother Peg reviews all that has happened to them in fulfillment of her own earlier dreams, and she prays for deliverance.

> PEG Dazed I am myself to be cursing her, and it all fore-shadowed that is coming to be. Dazed I am myself, for isn't the brain stopped from working inside my head, and no more they do be coming to me now, the forebodings, the tokens, and the dreams. 'Tis the same as if the end of all things was at hand, and I heard around me the crumbling of the world ... Holy Mary, Mother of God, pray for us sinners! ... Now and at the hour of death! ... Now and at the hour of death! (II, 147)

We hear these sentiments only from the two mothers, Ellen and Peg, who serve as an ironic chorus to the play, ironic because all their talk about omens and providence seems unrelated to the real substance of the play which involves human will, human action, and its consequences. The supernatural order is adverted to in *The Moonlighter,* but it does not actually intrude nor does it seem to have power over men's actions.

Power in this play is in the hands of men. Peter Guerin's pride causes him to send away his sons and there is a real moral gap of several generations between his own fierce nationalism in his youth and his utter intolerance of the national spirit in his sons. He has no sense that his own past may have been an inspiration to his sons. He is always sensitive to what people will think and this need for respectability makes him indifferent to human suffering. His son Eugene, following his father's history, has become a patriot. Peter Guerin's lack of sympathy for the cause leads Eugene after a year away from home to return a carbon copy of the elder Guerin. Peter's sense of what he has wrought in his last remaining son shocks him into a desperate and fatal act of courage. The phrase he repeats several times to Tom before they both go out to be cut down by the police—"my poor fellow"—has the same emotional impact as Lear's solicitude for his fool when he urges him in out of the storm. Both represent moments of moral growth and sympathetic contact with others. Neither man is as isolated as he was.

Peter Guerin first appears as a high-principled man concerned about his reputation in the community. Malachi says of Peter early in the play, "Obstinate as he is in points about principles and conduct, in the general way of acting according to custom no man is more tender of what the people do be saying of him than Peter Guerin." (II, 101) And Peter himself declares a bit later,

> It is tired I am of saying it, but I'm telling there's going to be a sudden stop put to the badgering between myself and Eugene. All of my name were big-spirited decent farmers that never done a mean or underhand act, and there was never a blackguard in my clan to match the sons I reared. But no blackguard will remain in my house to shame me before the world, and before the week is out Eugene will get the cost for a distant place. (II, 103)

Peter's assertion of high principle is challenged when we learn that he has been a "rentwarner" and has served the rent notices of absentee landlords for years. Raising of the rent enabled the large landholder to increase his land at the expense of the common people. It was against such exploitative procedures that the national movement was directed. Peter Guerin's participation in this disgraceful enterprise cancels out the admiration his sons had for him as a former Fenian.

Politics, of course, is a constantly corrupting force in *The Moonlighter*. It matters not whether one is pro-nationalism or anti-nationalism. The results are violence, suffering, and alienation. No amount of feeling about a cause should prompt a father to disown his son or a son to curse a father. And yet this happens. Peter rages at Eugene's militance and cries, "Go along, you naked scamp, and look for the grace of God! And leave my house, all of you—blackguards, refuse, and dirty murdering moonlighters, leave my house!" (II, 129) His son retorts,

> The grass will be growing to your doorstep before I come back to you—you that has kept me from my part in the work that will be done to-night for the glory of the nation.
>
> PETER Isn't that satisfaction enough for you for you to know that this glorious work will be done for the good of the nation?
>
> EUGENE There is no more to be said between me and you! But I'll leave you a keepsake to bear me in mind when I am far from home—I leave you my curse! (II, 131)

Never a humble man, Peter Guerin has no remorse when his son leaves, claiming that he has done his "duty" for Eugene. *King Lear* comes to mind once again as one thinks of Lear, Cordelia, and "duty."

Even after his son Eugene has been away for a year, Peter Guerin's feelings have not changed. Ellen Guerin looks forward to her son's homecoming with gladness in her heart, but Peter can only declare, "He'll get his shake-hands, and he'll get his welcome. And better than either, won't he be getting the land?" (II, 134) Only when his son actually returns and Peter listens to his empty language, does Peter realize his responsibility for what has happened. His silence is eloquent, as Eugene makes it more and more evident that he has lost his soul and his heart in the big city. Tom Driscoll's arrival prompts Peter to make a desperate and futile attempt to help him. Just before he runs out of the house to be gunned down by the police, Peter Guerin admits his responsibility for what has happened and recovers his moral freedom.

> PETER Ah, my fine young man, to be riddled by the police—the black cowards that shot down the men of Ireland when myself and his uncle Martin stood shoulder to shoulder in the Fenian days! Sure he was no blackguard, and deceived I was in my pride when I called them black-

guards all the fine young men of these latter times. And will I let him—the nephew of my staunchest friend—be riddled by the police! [*takes up gun*] The dirty police! [*goes out*] (II; 148)

Fitzmaurice has built a structure of emotions in *The Moonlighter* which makes the final moments of the play almost unbearable, the way that the conclusions of *The Plough and the Stars* and *Juno and the Paycock* are unbearable. Whatever the justice, the human loss is tremendous. No political explanation can make reasonable the deaths of such men. Those who remain—again the Lear analogy is apt—are those with less ample hearts and souls. Breeda's lament over the dead Tom Driscoll at the very end of the play is intensely moving and a fine example of poetic dialect as a medium for the expression of feeling. The extended rhythms build her sorrow into a keening lament.

BREEDA He is gone now, and I'm too late to tell him my heart throbbed only for him, only for him all the time, and I deceiving myself in my folly and my pride. Even in this hour the hardness was in my heart the time he passed me with the gun, and I never knowing the trouble that was on him, or that he was going to his death. And I scorned the one appealing look he gave me. One appealing look he gave me and then walked on so cold and proud. My God! to let him to his death with never a word from me to soften for him the bitter pain. Oh, Jesus! what put the film in my eyes? Oh, Jesus! what put the film in my eyes? Now let not a hair remain in this head! Let the prongs of fire come down from the heavens and scorch me to the ground! (II, 150)

Turning from *The Moonlighter* to *The Country Dressmaker,* we move in the realistic plays from tragedy to the conventional comedy which was Fitzmaurice's first Abbey play. It opened on October 3, 1907 with an excellent cast that included many of the Abbey regulars, Sara Allgood as Julia Shea; Frank Fay as Matt Dillane; Arthur Sinclair as Michael Clohesy; J. M. Kerrigan as Pats Connor; and Willie Fay as Luke Quilter, the man from the mountains. It has been, as I have pointed out in chapter 1, one of the Abbey's most-revived plays and without question the best known of George Fitzmaurice's plays. *The Country Dressmaker* is not as true to the experience of North Kerry as are Fitzmaurice's later plays and I think a problem he faced all of his life was whether to write to please an audience or to write what he knew to be true. More often he did the latter, and it cost him critical recognition.

To say that *The Country Dressmaker* is a conventional comedy is not to deny its effectiveness, for it is an extremely well-made play. In it, however, folk elements are less important than comic forms. *The Country Dressmaker* could be about any rural Irish family and indeed about almost any rural family at all. Its theme is a traditional one, namely, that a foolish young lady who bases her expectations about love on what she reads in romances has to learn the hard way that love and marriage involve compromise and coming to terms with reality.

The combination of sufficiently distanced but believable characters and a sensible lesson about the dangers of dreaming makes for a good comedy and, I think, explains the popularity of *The Country Dressmaker*. Nothing here to surprise one, no loose ends, nothing terribly strange, simply an evening's entertainment. In his later plays, as we have seen, George Fitzmaurice was not content merely to repeat the formulas of comedy.

He attempted to get closer to the realities of life in North Kerry, to its violence, its brutality, its lyricism, and its folk beliefs. These later plays are also closer to Fitzmaurice's own imaginative world, a world where there is far more room for the dreamer than there is in the familiar world of *The Country Dressmaker.* But, as I have suggested earlier in this study, such plays were not nearly so comprehensible to the Dublin theatergoer, or to the critics, or, indeed, to Yeats and Lady Gregory. Ironically, Fitzmaurice wrote folk-plays which were too close to the real experience of folk. He got little hearing for these plays.

The Country Dressmaker concerns the fortunes of Julia Shea, the dressmaker of the title, who has for ten years been faithfully awaiting the return of Pats Connor from America. She is convinced that Pats went abroad to earn enough money so they could lead a comfortable married life. Her hopes are sustained by mention of her in letters which Pats writes to his friends the Clohesys, though Julia has received no letters from him herself. Julia's family is convinced she is headed for spinster-hood and so they engage a "mountainy man," Luke Quilter, who has had much experience as a matchmaker, to bring Julia to her senses. Another suitor, Edmund Normyle is on hand and deeply in love with Julia. Quilter, more civilized and good-humored than his counterpart Morgan Quille in *The Magic Glasses,* confronts Julia with the prospects of a lonely old age and has almost succeeded in winning her over to Normyle's suit when Pats Connor's whistle is heard outside the door and all bets are off.

In the second act the scene shifts to the Clohesy farm

where Michael Clohesy is making plans to inveigle Pats
Connor into marrying one of his own daughters, Babe or
Ellie. Clohesy considers his daughters a good match for
Pats because his family, since it owns land, is higher in
the rural social hierarchy than the Sheas, who are landless tenants rather than farmers. During Act II we learn
that Julia has been deceived all these years by one of the
Clohesy sisters, who has only pretended to have received
letters from Pats Connor which spoke of his love for
Julia Shea. We learn too that Pats has not been idle in
America, but has, during his stay there, married a Ger-
man woman who has subsequently died under mysterious circumstances. Pats really has no special fondness
for either of the Clohesy girls, and, when he learns of
the tricks they have played on Julia, he determines to
make Julia's dream come true. He declares his love to
Julia, she is transported, and events appear to be headed
for a happy ending. What has not been resolved, of
course, is their mutual unawareness. Julia doesn't know
about Pats's former life; Pats is unaware of Julia's senti-
mentality.

Act III brings both Pats and Julia into a more realistic
awareness of each other and concludes with a decision
"to make the best of it," and to get married anyway.
During Act III Julia admits that Pats does not live up to
the romantic image of a lover she had formed from her
romances. She also learns of Pat's previous marriage and
realizes that he is no longer the innocent and chaste
hero she has sought. And Pats learns that Julia is no
saint either, when she impulsively sends a note to the
hapless Edmund Normyle on the day of his wedding.
Despite these discoveries, Pats and Julia decide to

marry. Luke Quilter calls the match "the most timorous job I ever put of me." (III, 57)

The most interesting character in *The Country Dressmaker* is Luke Quilter, who, like Morgan Quille in *The Magic Glasses,* is one of Fitzmaurice's "mountainy men." Luke's character, unlike others in the play, is firmly rooted in North Kerry. Fitzmaurice probably knew such characters in Listowel or Abbeyfeale. John B. Keane, who lives in the same area, has created a similar character in Pats Bo Bwee in his play *Sharon's Grave.* Pats was a well-known quack in the Listowel area and Keane has masterfully brought him to life in the play. There is a Falstaffian quality about these "mountainy men;" they can't be reduced to a descriptive phrase. Julia Shea is clearly the "starry-eyed dreamer" who must learn that life always involves settling for less. Pats Connor is the "returned Yank," self-reliant to a fault. But Luke Quilter is not simply the "matchmaker." Indeed, as a matchmaker he is pretty much a failure. He arrives to make a case for Edmund Normyle and succeeds in preparing Julia for Pats Connor. With a pragmatic determination to be at all costs on the winning side, Luke quickly tacks about and ends up persuading Julia that she and Pats are right for each other!

Luke enters the Shea kitchen in Act I and immediately dominates the scene with his combination of blather and good sense.

LUKE God bless the woman of the house! . . . Put the hand there, brown Matthew. My dear man, it isn't a grey rib you have in the whisker and you turned sixty. And it's as hardy as a jack-shipe you are yourself, Norry Shea. (III,21)

Luke's first strategy with Julia is to undermine her romantic self-assurance with a homely reminder that no beauty lasts forever. "Age!", he says, "Age is a woeful and terrible misfortune." (III,24)

Luke follows this bit of "crossness" with a bit of "love" calculated to raise the rather ordinary Edmund Normyle to the idealized level of Julia's sensibility. Fitzmaurice spins off this bit of lyricism effortlessly and unselfconsciously, unlike his heavy-handed efforts with the American dialect of Pats Connor.

> LUKE It's of love we'll be talking . . . It's to tell you about this man I want. Your heart would soften if it was of flint itself if you knew the way he does be above in Cornamona. When the day's grand with the sun shining above in the heavens he do be in great wind, and hope and joy be in him. It's smiling like a half-fool he does be to himself and he listening to the thrushes and blackbirds and robineens singing in the little crough below the house, for it's your own voice he thinks he hears amongst them and they making ceol . . . But when the day is dull and chilly and the grey rain comes fleeping down Knockroe, he do be lonesome in himself and not a word out of him, he thinking then somehow that your heart is sealed against him and that 'twill never change. (III,26)

I immediately think of Synge when I come across passages like this in Fitzmaurice. The cadences flow beautifully despite the unfamiliar syntax. And the participles seem to catch the sense as it sails down to a close and give it a whirl again upward—"and he listening to the thrushes and the robineens singing," "and they making ceol," "he thinking then somehow." The effect is like a musical coda which gives a bit more turn to the phrase just when one thinks the song is done. Synge made a reputation out of the faithful rendering of this

quality in peasant talk. Fitzmaurice, who grew up in the places he writes of, uses such beguiling lyricism only occasionally, probably because he knew it was only occasionally heard in real peasant speech. Paradoxically, this authentic folk-dramatist had his feet fixed too firmly to the ground to write the sort of sustained idealization of peasant speech which made Synge famous.

One reason that a "mountainy man" like Luke Quilter can move so freely in this comic world is that he exists outside the class structure of the society. Fitzmaurice, as I have noted earlier, grew up painfully aware of the difference between gentry, clergy, and commoner, as well as between Roman Catholic and Church of Ireland. In the country the rigid social hierarchy distinguished the landed from the landless, the owner-farmer from the tenant-farmer. Upward mobility was the exception rather than the rule. One could free himself from the strictures of social hierarchy by leaving the land, as Pats Connor does, and returning with his fortune made. It was assumed that anyone returning to the country from America must have had good fortune. As Min Dillane says, "there's nothing thought of the next-door neighbours. It's the people far away." (III,19) Pats began as an orphan, so his rise has been an unusual one indeed.

In the social hierarchy of *The Country Dressmaker* the Sheas are lower than the Clohesys, a fact which makes Julia's romantic fantasies of Lady Gwendolen and Sir Geoffrey even more foolish. Both families farm, but the Sheas appear to be tenant-farmers who have been evicted from time to time, while the Clohesys own their farm. The Clohesys view themselves as "big

people," clearly superior to the Sheas. Matt Dillane refers to them early in the play as "the big clan now in the parish." (III,20) When the Clohesys invade the Shea's house in Act III to persuade Pats Connor that he's making a mistake in marrying Julia Shea, their argument follows strictly along class lines. The Sheas are not good enough for him. Michael Clohesy has grand plans for the social rise of Pats Connor. "I told them about the Yank and all to that, and how I wanted to bring him here and there among them and they big people, J. P.'s, District Councillors, Publicans, and so forth, till it would get stuck in him how fine and wealthy they were." (III,32-3) Clohesy, of course, views Pats as a means to his own social advancement.

Having discussed at some length now Fitzmaurice's best comedy, we can proceed to a less successful effort in the genre, *'Twixt the Giltinans and the Carmodys.* Lennox Robinson produced *'Twixt the Giltinans and the Carmodys* at the Abbey in 1923, hoping, no doubt, to capitalize on the popularity of *The Country Dressmaker,* which this play resembles in plot, characterization, and incident. The cast included such Abbey regulars as Arthur Shields, who played Billeen Twomey; Michael J. Dolan, who played Michael Clancy; and F. J. McCormick, who played Simon Giltinan. The play had a run of ten performances and was not revived. *The Country Dressmaker* is superior to *'Twixt the Giltinans and the Carmodys* because its plot has a logical inevitability which does not rely on external devices to motivate action. Its characters and incidents are also more interesting. Howard K. Slaughter states that *'Twixt the Giltinans and the Carmodys* was begun in 1919, but our

knowledge about the composition of Fitzmaurice's plays is extremely limited. Fitzmaurice may very well have written the play much earlier than this, perhaps even before *The Country Dressmaker.* This hypothesis would make much more sense of the great differences in quality between the two plays, but there is no way we can know for certain when the play was written.

Both *The Country Dressmaker* and *'Twixt the Giltinans and the Carmodys* involve the efforts of a matchmaker to splice unwilling middle-aged characters. The "returned Yank" figures centrally in both plays, and he is presumed by his neighbors to be wealthy and therefore worthy. Both of these "returned Yanks" end up married or about to be married to disillusioned and grudging women who themselves have discovered serious flaws in the character of the reputed hero. Violence, lyricism, and the supernatural have been muted in both plays, thus making them both more like conventional comedies and less like folk-plays.

Michael Clancy, the matchmaker in *'Twixt the Giltinans and the Carmodys,* has been trying for fifteen years to get Billeen Twomey to choose between two presumably once-fair ladies, Bridie Giltinan and Madge Carmody. Billeen, now forty, lived for a time in Chicago and became, so the story goes, a millionaire. He keeps several locked chests in his bedroom. At wit's end about how to get Billeen married and thus collect his fee, Clancy concocts a story about the plans of a mysterious Tomaus Brack "to slaughter [Billeen] if he isn't married for himself by five o'clock." (III,79) Much of the play concerns the arrival of, first, the Giltinans, and then the Carmodys, for a final round with the circumspect Billeen. Despite his fear of Brack's imminent wrath, Billeen puts off a decision between Bridie and Madge and sends them off to await his final word. Unfortunately for the matchmaker, the two families meet each other as they leave the house and they return to settle the score with Billeen. But they are less able to deal with each other than they are with Billeen and a nasty brawl erupts which Michael Clancy breaks up with a "four-prong pike." By now it's almost five o'clock and doomsday for Billeen Twomey.

Fortunately there is another eligible woman on stage, Old Jane, the serving girl, who turns out to be not so old after all and eager to share Billeen's fortune. So a match is made with proper words pronounced by a priest of questionable credentials who quite literally comes out of the woodwork. Immediately after the exchange of vows, Old Jane heads for the treasure chests, only to discover, of course, that there is no million at all, just a few hundred pounds. At this point, all both of them can do is to make the best of it and they engage in an exploratory kiss as the curtain falls.

A comparison of *'Twixt the Giltinans and the Carmodys* with *The Country Dressmaker* reveals several ways in which the latter is a better play. Fitzmaurice carefully keeps violence and the supernatural, qualities which define his folk-plays, out of *The Country Dressmaker*. They are present in *'Twixt the Giltinans and the Carmodys,* but awkwardly present, serving as handy devices with which to motivate action rather than organic elements in a coherent dramatic world. Thus, Michael Clancy's threat to bring down upon Billeen the vengeance of Tomaus Brack finally motivates Billeen to marry

Old Jane, but never exists for the audience as anything more than a *deus ex machina.* No Hag of Barna appears, no Linnaun Shee. It's all in Michael Clancy's imagination, yet the language would be appropriate for *The Dandy Dolls* or *The Linnaun Shee,* where such creatures really have power over men and where there is therefore a correlation between language and feeling.

> CLANCY [*pointing at window, in hollow tones*] Will you have time, anyway, and Tomaus moving southwards. The big black head of him is above the brow of that little hill, now.
> BILLEEN A reek of turf a head? Finuicane's reek and I know it.
> CLANCY [*evenly*] The hearse plumes shaking—the hearse plumes Tomaus dons when the blood-lust is maddening him. Deluded and blinded you are for faith 'tisn't the like of them would be shaking on a reek of turf, my poor man.
> BILLEEN [*overwhelmed with terror*] Plumes and not rushes! The murder, 'tis him! I don't want to be slaughtered and I'm ready, Michael Clancy. (III, 95)

Fitzmaurice omits such external devices entirely from *The Country Dressmaker,* making it closer, as I have said, to pure comedy rather than to folk-drama.

Several other points of comparison between the two plays can be made, with *The Country Dressmaker* consistently the superior play. Fitzmaurice dramatizes the social hierarchy in *'Twixt the Giltinans and the Carmodys* in the rivalry between the two families for Billeen. The Giltinans are spoken of as having "grace," the Carmodys as "rogues," but the playwright does not work out the class difference in detail as he does in *The Country Dressmaker.* Neither does he create in Michael Clancy a Luke Quilter. Clancy functions simply as a

matchmaker and Fitzmaurice does not give him the gift
of dialect and place which transforms Luke into a believable character. Finally, the conclusion of *'Twixt the
Giltinans and the Carmodys* relies on the unlikely alli-
ance between Billeen and Old Jane, whom Fitzmaurice
seems to have kept on stage just for this purpose. Far
more dramatically appropriate is the resolution of *The
Country Dressmaker,* where Julia, a blend of Bridie and
Madge, swallows her pride and accepts her deflated lover
for what he really is.

I want to turn now from this minor comedy to two
important plays which George Fitzmaurice wrote as an
old man and which have been almost entirely neglected.
One Evening Gleam was published in *The Dublin Magazine* in 1949 and produced by Liam Miller at the Studio
Theatre Club in 1952. *The Coming of Ewn Andzale*
appeared in *The Dublin Magazine* in 1954 and has never
been produced. It was probably Fitzmaurice's last play.
These two plays deserve a better fate because they represent the playwright going in significant new directions.
Both plays are set in Dublin rather than North Kerry
and both reflect the quality of life which Fitzmaurice
observed in his many years there. The plays have a pessi-
mistic view of human possibilities in a world that has
lost contact with the visionary gleam.

One Evening Gleam is a very short one-act play which,
unlike most of Fitzmaurice's plays, has little plot. Two
of his most recurrent preoccupations, violence and the
supernatural, are relegated to the periphery of the play,
as Fitzmaurice concerns himself with the consciousness
and feelings of ordinary, rather dull-witted people who
are preoccupied with the dull routine of Dublin life. A

most remarkable event occurs at the end of the play—a blind man suddenly sees and just as suddenly drops dead. The speakers observe the event and remark that it had been predicted just such a thing would happen, but this is noted with scarcely a ripple of personal involvement and the speakers go back to their previous empty conversation.

The play has a disorienting effect, something like that achieved by Degas in his revolutionary painting, *The Glass of Absinthe,* in which the figures are off-centered and the subject runs off the canvas past the formal boundary of the frame. The play also reminds me of similar developments in the novel, in Fitzmaurice's time with Ford Maddox Ford, and in our own time with Lawrence Durrell, where the narrator of the novel has neither an accurate grasp of the facts nor much awareness of their significance. The quality of emptiness which the drab conversation communicates also suggests the world of Samuel Beckett. His play *Come and Go* also involves three women who do nothing more than gossip and backbite and whose prattle has nothing in it of intensity, commitment, lyricism, or even violence. Headpieces filled with straw.

One Evening Gleam has only four characters and takes place in a Dublin apartment. Mrs. Agnes Cleary and Mrs. Nancy Hannigan are the two old women whose conversation takes up most of the play. Phoebe Tollemache, a parson's daughter and a spinster, lives upstairs. Mrs. Cleary's son Jim, forty years old and blind since the age of five, lies asleep in the room during all but the last few moments of the play.

The play opens with Mrs. Cleary and Mrs. Hannigan

discussing the implications of the doctor's recent visit to Jim. Rather matter-of-factly, Mrs. Hannigan recalls the prediction made by "that old Aygyptian you took him to twenty years ago" that Jim would die the instant he recovered his sight. (III, 61) Little is made of this incredible bit of supernaturalism, which, of course, is fulfilled at the end of the play. Conversation turns instead to the parson's daughter and her unorthodox ways. Agnes and Nancy exchange gossip about whether or not she is really a parson's daughter, about her strange comings and goings, and about her flirtatious behavior toward Jim, yet exceedingly prudish behavior with the old bachelor who lives upstairs. Talk then turns to Mrs. Cleary and Mrs. Hannigan themselves and how their lives in Dublin have really been more exciting than that of Miss Tollemache with her highfalutin ways. "It's a fancy name she has got anyway—Phoebe Tollemache, like a concoction you'd make out from a book." (III, 63)

Phoebe arrives at this point and we begin to realize more and more that we are not getting an accurate picture of reality from Mrs. Cleary and Mrs. Hannigan. Phoebe has the wit to lead both of them along nicely. And she brings out some things about the two old women which they had been concealing from each other, such as Mrs. Hannigan's "boozing" and Mrs. Cleary's talent as a pickpocket. Fitzmaurice reminds us that no one is being quite honest in this play nor does anyone understand what is happening or about to happen.

Just before Phoebe departs, the subject of the Egyptian's doctor's prediction comes up again and

Phoebe declares the doctor wasn't Egyptian at all, but Indian. She pauses for a bit to muse "sometimes those Orientals have mysterious ways of penetrating things," then glances at Jim's bed and comments, "He seems all right, except being a little flushed." (III, 74) Phoebe leaves and the two old women wait for Jim to wake. Jim wakes, cries out, "Mother!" and "I see the moon, I see the moon!", and then dies. His mother notes that it wasn't really the moon he saw at all, but the gleam from an old lamp. The women then exchange an ironic "God bless" as the curtain falls. Nothing is as it appears to be.

What would *One Evening Gleam* have been, we wonder, had it been told from Jim's point of view or Phoebe's or even from that of the doctor who examined the blind man just before the play opens. Phoebe states at one point "what really mattered was what was going on within oneself and . . . your whole world so to speak, is contained between the sole of the foot and the occiput." (III, 69) In this play we never really know what is going on in people's head, just what they will risk telling about themselves.

Surrounding everything in this unsettling play is the power of pre-science and magic which raises doubts about the efficacy of the final "God bless." Magic is encountered regularly in Fitzmaurice's Kerry plays, but there the people seem more accustomed to it and at least one character in a play has contact with the supernal powers. Fitzmaurice seems to be implying that life in the city dulls the sensibility and removes one from contact with the fairies and their power. Jim may very well have seen the moon, but all his mother and friend can see is the gleam of the old lamp.

Before leaving *One Evening Gleam,* I want to raise the question of its relation to Fitzmaurice's own life and family. Phoebe's character, for example, might have been suggested by one of Fitzmaurice's spinster sisters. She would also have been a parson's daughter, a Protestant, and fairly well-to-do. Somewhat eccentric, she would have been an easy mark for the insensitive and envious jibes of less well-off Roman Catholic neighbors. One habit which drives Mrs. Cleary wild is Phoebe's habit of playing the "pianner." She is playing at the moment of Jim's vision and death. Fitzmaurice's sisters were known to entertain guests with piano music. Another thing which puzzles the two Dublin ladies is Phoebe's regular disappearance from the city every three months or so. Fitzmaurice could certainly understand this need to get away from the city, something he did regularly himself. Finally, an old bachelor lives upstairs over Mrs. Cleary and she suspects he is a Protestant as well and thus fair game for Miss Tollemache.

MRS. CLEARY 'Tisn't her at all after all but that oul' bachelor man that lives on the tip-top. He has a noisy step like Phoebe.

MRS. HANNIGAN Another mystery, her fad or her foible or whatever you'd call it about Jim here and she takes no notice of th' oul' bachelor man that would suit her down to the ground. She'd pass him up and down the stairs forty times in the day and never give him the glad eye. And, I don't know but he's a prodestant.

MRS. CLEARY He's a woman hater. You didn't know that.

MRS. HANNIGAN I did not. But she must know it. Didn't I tell you there wasn't a thing in the world but that dickens of a woman finds out.

MRS. CLEARY 'Tis your crony Mrs. Durcan that told me about it. Th' ould bachelor man was jilted in his young days. He's a Corkman and they say they never forgive a thing like that down in that part of the world. (III, 65)

Fitzmaurice was also a bachelor who lived in a Dublin apartment and who may indeed have been jilted in his youth. A Corkman is not a Kerryman, but precise locations tend to get fuzzy from the olympian perspective of a Dubliner!

The Coming of Ewn Andzale is a puzzling play which one is tempted to call a failure. One recent critic, J. D. Riley, who has no hesitancy about putting Fitzmaurice at his best on a level with O'Casey and Synge, calls this play "the only real failure among Fitzmaurice's plays." It is certainly a different sort of Fitzmaurice play. Dialect is gone completely and what Robert Hogan calls a language of "polite formality" has replaced it. The play is not set in Kerry, but in Monkstown, a suburb of Dublin. Fitzmaurice tells us we are in the drawing room of the Davenport family which, to judge from the furnishings, is comfortably middle-class. The play deals with the return of the native, a plot Fitzmaurice has used before, most successfully in *The Country Dressmaker*. And the play's characters are a dull lot, without a Luke Quilter or a Morgan Quille among them. All of this adds up to a pretty mediocre effort, certainly not vintage Fitzmaurice.

Why would Fitzmaurice write such a play? He knew perfectly well that a Fitzmaurice play without dialect and without Kerry characters was risky. No doubt he had to work over the drawing-room conversations in *The Coming of Ewn Andzale* much more than he did his native Kerry speech or even the Dublin dialect which seems to flow so naturally in *One Evening Gleam*. And the result was still such a stiff and self-conscious speech that he was probably never satisfied with it himself. And yet he had the play published.

I think Fitzmaurice was trying to accomplish something in *The Coming of Ewn Andzale* which required him to forsake dialect and the country, and concentrate on the experience of an educated, middle-class, urban, probably Protestant, Anglo-Saxon family. His most moving earlier plays—*The Magic Glasses, The Linnaun Shee, The Dandy Dolls, The Green Stone*—suggest a certain kind of Irish consciousness, spontaneous, close to nature, in touch with supernatural powers. No one, not even the priest in the community, doubts the presence of the fairies, which indeed manifests itself violently in each of the plays.

In *The Coming of Ewn Andzale,* however, another kind of Irish consciousness appears, one which is removed from the land, one in which orthodox education has replaced natural lore, and faith in the fairies has become faith in reason and empiricism. And yet events in the play belie this "modern" consciousness and suggest that mysterious powers are still at work in human life, even though no one in the play has more than a glimmer of awareness. The very name of the play, *The Coming of Ewn Andzale,* suggests the coming of those other creatures like the Linnaun Shee or the Hag of Barna or that fire-and-brimstone devil who claims Jaymony Shanahan in *The Magic Glasses.*

The Coming of Ewn Andzale is about the Davenport family, once fairly prosperous but now, because of certain stock reverses, rather down on its luck. The furnishings of their drawing room, where the action takes place, include a gramophone, a piano, books, an ottoman, two chairs, and a sofa. Clearly, the Davenports are not poor. The play opens with "Captain" Davenport—

Fitzmaurice never indicates why he has this title—assuring his family that the arrival of Ewn Andzale is imminent, within the half hour. Mrs. Davenport has apparently received from such a person a letter that promises to save the Davenports from financial ruin. Their daughter Queenie arrives and immediately sets about discrediting the Ewn Andzale story with the suggestion that Mrs. Davenport, being slightly mad anyway, has made the whole thing up, even to the point of fabricating the "letter." Ewn Andzale, Queenie triumphs, is simply an anagram for "New Zealand." Mrs. Davenport happens to be fond of crosswords.

Just when Queenie has almost convinced everyone that the whole thing is a hoax, a loud knocking is heard at the door followed by a scream. Not Ewn Andzale, though, just Bridget the maid terrified by a mouse. Someone has arrived, however, and it is Uncle Silas, Mrs. Davenport's half-brother who has for years been away in New Zealand. Silas reads the Ewn Andzale letter and offers to make the arrangement come true. The family celebrates its good fortune and Mrs. Davenport realizes that the prediction has come true. If Uncle Silas wasn't Ewn Andzale when he arrived, he certainly metamorphosed in short order.

Fitzmaurice's primary purpose in writing *The Coming of Ewn Andzale* was to portray the Irish family cut off from the land and from religious, cultural, and mythic traditions. We learn early in the play that the Davenports have been driven off their land by the depradations of the Sinn Feiners, and are now "reduced to pinching and scraping in this little suburban house in Monkstown driven even to the deplorable extreme of

having to take in those bed-and-breakfast people."
(III, 146) They have lost contact with folk traditions
which enrich the lives of Kerry peasants. Queenie, their
"educated" daughter, about whom more later, speaks
cynically about fairy tales and their origin, and her
words reveal the loss of innocence which Fitzmaurice
knew to be the product of civilization.

> QUEENIE As well as the rest of you, I have read that letter
> to mother from an individual signing himself, herself, or
> itself Ewn Andzale. At first, I said to myself this is really
> too good to be true and then I began to reflect on the
> origin of the so-called fairy tales . . . I mean those tales con-
> ceived ages ago when the world was young, the authorship
> of which is unknown . . . The motive or aspiration in every
> one of those fairy tales is the very same as that behind the
> wording of this letter from Ewn Andzale—namely, a wish to
> by-pass by some fluke or other the intolerable and seem-
> ingly unjust workings of fate. The wish in the fairy tales
> represented an emanation from the subconscious self which
> is also the case in this letter from Ewn Andzale. (III, 147)

Mrs. Davenport, the person in the play closest to the
old traditions, is reputed to have seen a satyr in her
youth, though her skeptical brother Silas belittles the
idea.

> SILAS I never knew her to do anything odd or strange or
> foolish, except once when she rushed into the house in a
> state of great excitement saying she had seen a real satyr—
> not a goat she said—but a real satyr in the corner of the Big
> Shrubbery . . . the Big Shrubbery was on a slope was dark-
> ish and had a certain awesome appearance about it.
> (III, 159)

The satyr, of course, would represent the world of fairy
and myth which has been educated and urbanized out
of the "modern" Irish consciousness.

The books which Mrs. Davenport keeps so neatly

stacked on the drawing room table are all religious tracts which have in common a dry rationalism far removed from the simple Roman Catholic faith of the Kerry folk. The books include "Pearson on the *Creed;* Paley on the *Origins of Christianity;* Moscheim's *Ecclesiastical History;* Woods' *Natural History* . . . Taylor's *Holy Living and Dying;* Hooker's *Sermons;* Latimer's *Preparation for Communion."* (III, 160) The titles prompt Silas to comment, "Is this a Plymouth Brother establishment or what?" (III, 160) Religious education through such books would quickly remove the emotional and imaginative dimensions of religious experience and seriously jeapordize the faith, as it obviously has for Queenie, who has turned from Christianity to Freud.

Silas, the newly returned brother, and Popham, the Davenports' son, also show signs of having lost touch with the folk tradition. Silas, who once possessed a distinctive Cockney accent, has carefully normalized his English, so much so that his sister cannot believe she is speaking to the same person.

SILAS In the far-off days when I used those aitches, which I should not have used, and did not use those aitches, which I should have used, and there was no help in me, Dympha used to call me her vulgar cockney half-brother, Silas . . . I was associated with a couple of University men when I first went to New Zealand, which did the trick for me, and having a good ear for music I managed to achieve a magnificent Hoxford and Cambridge accent, unlike the Higginbotham family who hailed from Islington that a battleship wouldn't knock out of the habit of saying "wiv" instead of with. (III, 157)

Popham's ambition is to be a garage mechanic and he intends to use his uncle's largesse to this end. There is a subtle irony here, I think, which relates to George Fitzmaurice's personal quirks. Liam Miller told me that George would never ride in any motorized transportation at all. His opinion of garage mechanics would therefore be especially low.

What all of this means, then, is that the Davenport family is rootless. It is humorless as well; laughter, when it does occur, is always at the expense of someone else. Queenie tries for laughs as she quite deliberately and cruelly attacks her mother's credibility. Queenie is identified early on in the play as a bluestocking "who doesn't believe in anything." (III, 145) Her intellectual idol would seem to be Freud, though Fitzmaurice provides no footnotes. She diagnoses her mother's condition in terms of the unconscious, projection, obsession, and transference. Unfortunately, Fitzmaurice doesn't quite make the Freudian dialect come off and consequently Queenie is not believable as a character. But his impatience with such a doctrinaire, scientific, unemotional, and unimaginative view of human experience reveals itself, I think, in the prolixity of Queenie's speech.

I think there is an irony in the conclusion of *The Coming of Ewn Andzale* just as there is in *The Green Stone,* another play about wish-fulfillment. In both plays the wishes of the protagonists come true and in both plays this results in more money for everyone, but no improvement in personal relations. In *The Coming of Ewn Andzale* the Davenport family is no closer together at the end of the play than it was at the beginning. Furthermore, separation from the folk tradition makes the family blind to the fact that a prophecy has been fulfilled after all. Ewn Andzale has arrived and dispensed gifts. It is never completely clear in the play that Queenie is right and that Mrs. Davenport fabricated the whole story. Quite obviously, some other supernatural force is at work. In Monkstown, however, the power cannot be named, but only given the identity of a cross-word anagram.

The Coming of Ewn Andzale was George Fitzmaurice's last play, begun in 1950 and published in 1954. How appropriate and sad that it should deal with an attenuation of the Irish folk consciousness so complete that not even one evening gleam from the other world manages to come through.

In this discussion of his realistic plays, I have challenged the idea that Fitzmaurice was a writer of comedies, or, more precisely, that he had a comic view of life. His comedies, especially *The Country Dressmaker,* are witty and well-made, and *The Country Dressmaker* has a splendid buffoon in Luke Quilter. But they are finally conventional efforts which I feel do not represent Fitzmaurice's most original and serious work. And yet what reputation Fitzmaurice had in the past rested almost wholly on *The Country Dressmaker,* certainly until his "rediscovery" by Clarke and Miller after World War II. Now, audiences are beginning to appreciate Fitzmaurice's folk-plays, and this appreciation will grow with more productions of these plays, especially in the provincial theaters. There, paradoxically, the familiar plays of Keane, and MacMahon will make George Fitzmaurice's world no longer seem so strange. But Fitzmaurice's reputation as a dramatist will not rest entirely on his folk-plays. In *The Moonlighter, One Evening Gleam,* and *The Coming of Ewn Andzale,* he has written three serious plays which dramatize the tedium and meaninglessness of life that has lost contact with the enchanted land, and which deserve more critical attention and performance than they have received.

4

Dramatic Experiments and Short Stories

This final chapter will deal briefly with *The Toothache, The King of the Barna Men, The Enchanted Land, Waves of the Sea,* and *The Simple Hanrahans,* five Fitzmaurice plays which are lesser works than those already considered, and with his short stories which are important chiefly because they suggest themes and characterizations for later comedies. The plays span George Fitzmaurice's career as a dramatist, the first two coming from the period of *The Country Dressmaker* and *The Moonlighter; The Enchanted Land* and *The Waves of the Sea* from the 1920s; and the last probably from the 1940s. The stories were published in Dublin weeklies from 1900 to 1907.

The Toothache is a very good one-act farce about the terrifying consequences of having a tooth problem in the days before national health. An early play, probably written before *The Country Dressmaker,* it concerns the ordeal of an Irish countryman with some bad teeth and only the village blacksmith to yank them out. Under-lying the farce are grim suggestions about the violence in human nature and its effect on society. Fitzmaurice was preoccupied with this theme. Morgan Quille in *The Magic Glasses* is a slightly more sophisticated version of Mulcair the blacksmith. The tough Clohesys bully their way through *The Country Dressmaker.* Clancy terrifies Bileen Twomey with "the big black head" of Tomaus Brack in *'Twixt the Giltinans and the Carmodys* after he has driven off the battling families with a four-pronged pike. Father James and Timmeen have at it with the Hag's Son in *The Dandy Dolls.* And violence is made ritual in *The King of the Barna Men.*

When Fitzmaurice tries to make a whole play out of the material of farce, as he does in *The King of the Barna Men,* the result is less successful than *The Tooth-ache.* The play stretches a potentially very funny situa-tion, a wrestling match, into three acts which begin in the house of the reigning champion, move to a field for some business with a hag and blue ointment, and con-clude with the battle itself, fought before Conacher, "King of Carraweira."

There are elements in *The King of the Barna Men* which are central to Fitzmaurice's imaginative and moral vision, such as the presence of violence in society, the operation of the fairy world in the world of men, the conflict of Christianity and non-Christian superna-turalism, the relation of Kerry to the legendary Kings of Ireland, the vigorous dialect of North Kerry. Fitz-maurice incorporated these elements more successfully in other plays which were shorter or which had more potential for plot and character. They do not make a successful play in *The King of the Barna Men.* Nonetheless, it would have been illuminating to see what the dedicated company headed by Eamon Keane made of the play in a 1967 production. Very likely it was produced as an "entertainment" with the emphasis on farcical elements such as the wrestling match, a very anti-heroic King, an absurdly loquacious retainer named Aeneas Canty, a tipsy Protestant bishop, and a nervous and self-conscious soon-to-be ex-champion. The play certainly offers opportunities for a creative director, since Fitzmaurice provides only the broadest outline of what's to be done.

The Enchanted Land, a three-act play, was published in the *Dublin Magazine* in 1957 and produced by Howard Slaughter in 1966 at the Mischler Theater in Pennsylvania. It represents a significant departure from the Fitzmaurice plays considered thus far. The subject matter and style vary so much from his other plays that one is hard put to date its composition. Very likely it is a play Fitzmaurice had been tinkering with for years before it was finally accepted for publication. Professor Slaughter suggests 1921 as the date of composition, but does not indicate why he chose this date. *The Enchanted Land* can be viewed either as an unfortunate lapse in the dramatist's vision and control of material, or as an interesting piece of experimental theater. It deals with the plight of Eithne, enchanted away from her husband King Aeneas and imprisoned under the sea. Included are a conniving twelve-toed mermaid, a magic ball of thread, and a most unheroic, stammering king.

Austin Clarke suggests that Fitzmaurice, long a devotee of the Dublin music-hall, may have been trying in

The Enchanted Land to introduce elements of the music-hall style into a play. Perhaps, like T.S. Eliot, he was searching for a dramatic form and language more accessible to the ordinary Dublin playgoer than those of his Kerry plays. Eliot, no longer interested in writing more interior monologues on the order of "Prufrock" and "Gerontion," wrote *Sweeney Agonistes,* a play just as raucous and unsubtle in relation to Eliot's other works as *The Enchanted Land* is to the other plays of Fitzmaurice. Hugh Kenner makes the intriguing suggestion that Eliot, also a lover of the music-hall review, was trying to adapt its style to a dramatic form. So we find in *Sweeney Agonistes* the same sort of melodrama, abrupt juxtaposition of styles, and lyrical banality that marks the *Enchanted Land.* Both artists, I think, were trying to find new ways of delighting an audience. That they both failed does not reduce the significance of their attempt.

Two more Fitzmaurice plays remain to be considered, *The Simple Hanrahans* and *The Waves of the Sea.* Neither play was either performed or published during the playwright's lifetime and both were discovered in manuscript form after Fitzmaurice's death. The plays are included in the Dolmen Press collected edition. *The Waves of the Sea* could have been treated either with Fitzmaurice's folk-plays or with his realistic plays, for it contains elements of both. Indeed its unusual combination of styles has prompted me to include it here among his dramatic experiments. It is probably an early play, written around 1920. *The Simple Hanrahans* is a late play, one with which Fitzmaurice was probably tinkering until the end of his life. It represents another effort like *The Enchanted Land* to bring something like music-hall style into formal comedy. Though he claimed he had long since given up on the legitimate stage, George Fitzmaurice never ceased dreaming about another commercial success like *The Country Dress-maker.*

The Waves of the Sea begins as a light comedy with one of Fitzmaurice's most often repeated themes, the effect of unexpected material good fortune on a group of Kerry peasants. But the play soon moves into darker comedy with the acknowledgment of supernatural forces at work in the world. It ends with an almost tragic intensity as a natural disaster manipulated by alien powers threatens both lives and land. The play possesses a strange intermingling of forms. Fitzmaurice does not, however, work the comic and tragic elements into a completely effective play. He never had much success with long plays, except for *The Moonlighter.* He could have ended *The Waves of the Sea* very effectively after Act I with dark forces revealed in the landscape of comedy. But then Fitzmaurice would have needed the sardonic laughter of a Samuel Beckett. An exuberant second act with an elaborately contrived *deus ex machina* to make things right does not erase the memory we have of an encounter with human suffering and alienation.

A review of George Fitzmaurice's work would be incomplete without some comment on his short stories which have been collected in a recent Dolmen Press edition under the title *The Crows of Mephistopheles.* The stories appeared in the weekly Irish press between 1900 and 1907. The last of them, then, was published the year that *The Country Dressmaker* was first performed at the Abbey. Apparently Fitzmaurice stopped writing fiction after this and concentrated on drama. There may be additional stories hidden away in the National Library archives, but in all likelihood these would also date from the first decade of the century.

The stories are interesting mainly as early suggestions of themes and forms which Fitzmaurice would work out more effectively in his plays. The most obvious example of a fictional version of a later play is a short story called "Maeve's Grand Lover," which has very nearly the same plot as *The Country Dressmaker.* Here Maeve instead of Julia is devoted to the reading of romances and rejects a rather dull boyfriend for the man of her dreams who turns out to be a rotter. All but two of the stories deal with matchmaking, courtship, and marriage, themes which are repeated in Fitzmaurice's comedies. None of the matchmakers is as fully developed as Luke Quilter, though like Luke they are ready to use any means to get their clients married.

A rigid social hierarchy prevails in the stories as it does in the plays. People are typically motivated by what the neighbors will think rather than by personal needs. A widower nearly loses love because no one would approve of his marrying a serving-girl. A forty-three-year-old spinster becomes eligible for marriage only when she gets title to her brother's land. A marriage is sacrosanct even if one has married the wrong girl in "Peter Fagan's Veiled Bride," or if a mother has been tricked into giving her blessing, as in "The Plight of Lena's Wooers"; or even if an impressionable young man has been convinced a girl has qualities which it turns out she doesn't have at all.

What is notably lacking in the stories, except for "The Crows of Mephistopheles," is the supernaturalism, grotesquerie, and sympathy of Fitzmaurice's folk-plays. The only sympathetic figures in the stories are the bashful suitors like poor Phil Reilly in "The Bashfulness of Philip Reilly," who cannot declare himself to his Katie until humiliated into it in her kitchen.

I find "The Crows of Mephistopheles," the last story in the collection and perhaps George Fitzmaurice's last short story, the best of the lot. The subject is simple enough, Michael Hennessy's problem of crows infesting his garden. He learns from his neighbor in the Great House that killing a few crows or stringing them up will keep away the live ones for a long time. What makes the story effective is the atmosphere Fitzmaurice creates around Michael and his problem. The first half has as much about darkness and demons as any of the folk-plays and is very well written. The opening sounds a bit like Conrad. "A tendency to upbraid fate – to brood over misfortunes rather than to immediately seek by what means they may be palliated or overcome – seems to be generally characteristic of the Celt."

The struggle of a farmer against crows may not seem to justify such profound sentiments as these, but Fitzmaurice manages to make Michael, the farmer, real, interesting, and the object of our sympathy. The crows, simply mentioned at first, take on a symbolical significance which is finally played out in a terrifying dream Michael has. The crows possess a consciousness which enables them to understand Michael's purposes. Michael's fearful dream reveals to him that the crows are allied to the devil. Here again is the darker side of Fitzmaurice's imagination which we have seen previously manifest in his folk-plays and the best of his realistic plays. The second half of the story seems contrived, unfortunately, and one has the sense that Fitzmaurice was once more trying to please an audience rather than to communicate his vision of a reality which is often puzzling, sometimes frightening, and almost never just.

The dark and problematic world of "The Crows of Mephistopheles" underscores a point which I have made frequently in this study. Fitzmaurice was most at home with folk-plays. *The Pie-Dish, The Dandy Dolls,* and *The Magic Glasses* capture North Kerry life with its darkness, its supernaturalism, its violence, its lyricism, and its dialect. Always there are the dreamer who has seen visions and the earthbound who resent the disturbance of their unimaginative and routine lives. Three of Fitzmaurice's best realistic plays, *The Moonlighter, One Evening Gleam,* and *The Coming of Ewn Andzale,* deal with life which has never believed in visions or life where the vision is gone. Fitzmaurice understood the darkness and loneliness of life as well as he did its wit and foolishness.

The single surviving photograph of George Fitzmaurice reminds us of the lighter side of Fitzmaurice's dramatic vision and befits the creator of Luke Quilter, Dermot Rue Mallarkey, Proud Aeneas Canty, and the enchanted lands. Fitzmaurice refused to let his picture be taken and this surviving photograph is clipped from a larger family photo. It is a very poor picture, but a marvelous emblem. George is looking straight out at us with a half-smile on his face and a large stetson pulled firmly down to his ears. The picture is cracked and out of focus and the figure appears to be fading away. A happy accident has placed him somewhere beyond reality with the Hag of Barna and the Linnaun Shee. The picture reminds me of the Cheshire Cat, except that in George Fitzmaurice's case it will be the hat rather than the smile which remains.

Selected Bibliography

WORKS BY GEORGE FITZMAURICE

Separate Editions

Five Plays. London and Dublin: Maunsel, 1914. Boston: Little, Brown, 1917.

> Included in this volume are: *The Country Dressmaker, The Moonlighter; The Pie-Dish; The Magic Glasses; The Dandy Dolls.*

The Country Dressmaker. Dublin: Maunsel and Roberts, 1921.

The Plays of George Fitzmaurice, Vol. 1, Dramatic Fantasies.

Intro. by Austin Clarke. Dublin: Dolmen Press, 1967. Chester Springs, Pa.: Dufour Editions, 1967.

> Included in this volume are: *The Magic Glasses; The Dandy Dolls; The Linnaun Shee; The Green Stone; The Enchanted Land; The Waves of the Sea.*

The Plays of George Fitzmaurice, Vol. 2, Folk Plays. Intro. by Howard K. Slaughter. Dublin: Dolmen Press, 1970. Chester Springs, Pa.: Dufour Editions, 1970.

> Included in this volume are: *The Ointment Blue or The King of The Barna Men; The Pie-Dish; The Terrible Baisht; There are Tragedies and Tragedies; The Moonlighter.*

The Plays of George Fitzmaurice, Vol. 3, Realistic Plays. Intro. by Howard K. Slaughter. Dublin: Dolmen Press, 1970. Chester Springs, Pa.: Dufour Editions, 1970.

Included in this volume are: *The Toothache; The Country Dressmaker; One Evening Gleam; 'Twixt the Giltinans and the Carmodys; The Simple Hanrahans; The Coming of Ewn Andzale.*

The Crows of Mephistopheles, and Other Stories. Ed. and with intro. by Robert Hogan. Dublin: Dolmen Press, 1970.
Included in this volume are: "Peter Fagan's Veiled Bride"; "Maeve's Grand Lover"; "The Plight of Lena's Wooers"; "Peter Praisin"; "The Disappearance of Mrs. Mulreany"; "The Bashfulness of Philip Reilly"; "Cupid and Cornelius"; "The Streel"; "The Crows of Mephistopheles."

Published in Periodicals

"Peter Fagan's Veiled Bride," *The Weekly Freeman,* March 17, 1900.

"Maeve's Grand Lover," *The Irish Weekly Independent and Nation,* Nov. 17, 1900.

"The Plight of Lena's Wooers," *The Weekly Freeman,* Dec. 15, 1900.

"Peter Praisin," *The Irish Weekly Independent and Nation,* June 1, 1901.

"The Disappearance of Mrs. Mulreany," *The Weekly Freeman,* Nov. 16, 1901.

"The Bashfulness of Philip Reilly," *The Weekly Freeman,* March 19, 1904.

"Cupid and Cornelius," *The Irish Weekly Independent and Nation,* May 10, 1906.

"The Streel," *The Weekly Freeman,* March 2, 1907.

"The Crows of Mephistopheles," *The Shanachie* 2 (Summer 1907).

"The Linnaun Shee, a Comedy in One Act," *Dublin Magazine,* First Series 2 (Oct. 1924): 194–206.

"The Green Stone, a Play in One Act," *Dublin Magazine,* New Series 1 (Jan.–March 1926): 33–50.

" 'Twixt the Giltinans and the Carmodys, a Drama," *Dublin Magazine,* New Series, 18 (Jan.–March 1943): 11-33.

"There are Tragedies and Tragedies, a Play in One Act,"
Dublin Magazine, New Series, 23 (July–Sept. 1948):
13-25.

"One Evening Gleam, a Play in One Act," *Dublin Magazine,* New Series 24 (Jan.–March 1949): 5–21.

"The Coming of Ewn Andzale, a Play in One Act,"
Dublin Magazine, New Series 29 (July–Sept.
1954): 20–40.

"The Terrible Baisht, a Play in One Act," *Dublin Magazine,* New Series 29 (Oct.–Dec. 1954): 14–34.

"The Enchanted Land, a Play in Three Acts," *Dublin Magazine,* New Series 32 (Jan.–March 1957): 6–35.

"The Toothache," *The Malahut Review* 1 (Jan. 1967)

SECONDARY SOURCES

Boyd, Ernest A. *Contemporary Drama of Ireland.* Boston:
Little, Brown, and Company, 1917.

> Has a chapter on "Later Playwrights" that ranks
> Fitzmaurice with Colum and Synge as a
> folk-dramatist.

Clarke, Austin. "The Dramatic Fantasies of George
Fitzmaurice." *Dublin Magazine,* n.s. 15 (April-June
1940): 9-14.

> A review of *The Magic Glasses* and *The Dandy
> Dolls* that maintains that Fitzmaurice found in his
> dramatic experiments what Yeats and Lady
> Gregory were looking for.

Conbere, John P. "The Obscurity of George Fitzmaurice."
Eire-Ireland 6 (Spring 1971): 17-26.

> Takes up again the unresolved problem of why the
> Abbey Theatre rejected *The Dandy Dolls.* Conbere
> suggests Yeats simply didn't appreciate
> Fitzmaurice's belittling of sacred Irish legend and
> myth.

Haynes, W. "Another Irish Dramatist." *Dial,* 13 September
1917, pp. 208-209.

Henderson, Joanne L. "Checklist of Four Kerry Writers: George Fitzmaurice, Maurice Walsh, Bryan MacMahon, and John B. Keane." *The Journal of Irish Literature* 1 (May 1972): 101-119.

> An exhaustive bibliography that has been, in the main, repeated here.

Hogan, Robert. "The Genius of George Fitzmaurice," *Drama Survey* 5 (Winter 1966-67): 199-212. Reprinted in Robert Hogan, *After the Irish Renaissance: A Critical History of Irish Drama Since the Plough and the Stars.* Minneapolis: University of Minnesota Press, 1967, pp. 164-75.

> A capsule review of all of Fitzmaurice's plays with persuasive suggestions about his central themes and use of dramatic forms.

Kennedy, Maurice. "George Fitzmaurice: Sketch for a Portrait." *Irish Writing,* no. 15 (June 1951), pp. 38-46.

Malone, Andrew E. *The Irish Drama.* New York: Benjamin Blom, 1965.

> Has a chapter on "The Folk Dramatists" that ranks Fitzmaurice with Synge, Lady Gregory, and Colum in the genre.

_____. "Rise of the Realistic Movement." In *The Irish Theatre,* ed. Lennox Robinson. New York: Macmillan and Co., 1939, pp. 89-105.

Miller, Liam. "Fitzmaurice Country." *The Journal of Irish Literature* 1 (May 1972): 77-89.

> A lively and personal essay about Fitzmaurice's life and work. Miller has produced Fitzmaurice plays and his Dolmen Press has recently published a four-volume edition of Fitzmaurice's works.

_____. "George Fitzmaurice: A Bibliographical Note." *Irish Writing,* no. 15 (June 1951), pp. 47-48.

O'hAodha, Michael. "Fitzmaurice and the Pie Dish." *The Journal of Irish Literature* 1 (May 1972): 90-94.

> A balanced essay that discourages a mythologizing of George Fitzmaurice.

Riley, J. D. "The Plays of George Fitzmaurice." *Dublin Magazine* 31 (January-March 1955): 5-19.

The most searching analysis of Fitzmaurice's plays yet to appear. Argues for his mastery of the techniques of drama.

Slaughter, Howard K. "Fitzmaurice and the Abbey." *Educational Theatre Journal* 22 (May 1970): 146-54.

Essentially a shortened version of his book on Fitzmaurice.

_____. *George Fitzmaurice and His Enchanted Land.* Dublin: Dolmen Press, 1972.

The best biography of Fitzmaurice that we have. Has an extremely useful glossary of the Anglo-Irish vocabulary in the plays, an identification of Anglo-Irish place names in the plays, and a listing of Abbey Theatre productions of Fitzmaurice plays from 1907-1969.

Wardle, Irving. "Reputations—XV: George Fitzmaurice." *London Magazine* 4 (February 1965): 68-74.

A fine essay that stresses the importance of Kerry and of Irish tradition in Fitzmaurice plays.